THE SEASON OF LIVING DANGEROUSLY

THE
SEASON
OF
LIVING
DANGEROUSLY

A Fan's Notes on Baseball's Strangest Season

ROBERT KOPECKY

Epigraph Books
Rhinebeck, New York

The Season of Living Dangerously: A Fan's Notes on Baseball's Strangest Season © 2021 by Robert Kopecky

Paperback ISBN 978-1-951937-98-0
Hardcover ISBN 978-1-951937-99-7
eBook ISBN 978-1-954744-00-4

Library of Congress Control Number 2021901909

Cover image by Ashley Landis/AP
Back cover/flap image by Max Bender
Author photo by Alex Kopecky
Book and cover design by Colin Rolfe

Epigraph Books
22 East Market Street, Suite 304
Rhinebeck, NY 12572
(845) 876-4861
epigraphps.com

*For my father, who first walked me up the stairs
into the sunlight of Wrigley Field*

"Our 2020 season taught us that when the nation faces crisis, the national game is as important as ever, and there is nothing better than playing ball."

—STATEMENT BY MAJOR LEAGUE BASEBALL, FEBRUARY 1, 2021

Contents

PART TWO: THE POSTSEASON

Preface

I HAVE BEEN a baseball fan since my father first took me to Wrigley Field and I began collecting Topps baseball cards, the backs of which were the source of almost everything I knew about baseball and baseball players. Over a lifetime of watching and reading about baseball, I have come to understand more about how the game is played and how players can meaningfully be evaluated and compared. I have developed a more nuanced appreciation for both the quotidian events that comprise the core of each game and the much rarer special or even unique occurrences that, like slot machine jackpots, punctuate our experiences of the game over the course of a season. And I now get player statistics from the infinitely more fulsome Baseball-Reference.com.

I have watched baseball change and have learned to question, and often reject, what I thought I understood about the game. Like many baseball fans, I have also grown frustrated with some of the ways the game has evolved, most particularly the ever-slower pace of play and the steady decline in the ratio of action to inaction on the field. But despite my quarrels with the game, my affection remains.

Before this year I had always taken for granted that the baseball season was equivalent to one of the laws of nature—it just arrived each spring with the same certainty as longer days. In 2020, though, nature turned on us in the form of a deadly global pandemic. Covid-19 has inflicted a brutal human cost in lives and livelihoods, and it has disrupted everyday life for Americans in numerous less significant ways. For me and many others, one of the greatest of those petty inconveniences was the loss of baseball.

Cancelling the beginning of the season was of course the right thing to do. But acknowledging that did not alleviate the depressing prospect of a summer without baseball. Once Major League Baseball and the players agreed they would try to stage a season, albeit one of only 60 games, like many other fans I had a variety of conflicting views about that course. And when baseball resumed, I realized that this would be the first year in many decades that I would not attend a single baseball game in person. This season was going to be different, as was my experience as a baseball fan.

And it *was* very different. A 60-game season necessarily upset the equilibrium of the game. Hitters' and pitchers' counting statistics (hits, home runs, wins, strikeouts) were rendered comparatively meaningless. And performance measures such as batting average or earned run average were skewed by the significantly reduced sample size. Pennant races were not the six-month battles of perseverance and attrition that we rely on to identify the best teams.

Games were played in empty ballparks with piped-in crowd noise and cardboard fans in the seats. Broadcasters called the action from studios often hundreds of miles away. Numerous games were cancelled due to team Covid-19 outbreaks. MLB implemented new rules to speed up play (including placing an automatic runner on second to begin each extra inning) and accommodate a proliferation of doubleheaders (shortening games to seven innings). The National League employed the designated-hitter rule for the first time. Finally, the postseason was expanded to allow over half the teams to participate, and the World Series was played for the first time at a neutral site.

On top of all that, the games were played in a summer of widespread civil unrest and protests against racial inequity in America, and major-league baseball players were, in a way never seen before, vocal and visible participants in expressing that message on and off the field. On one occasion during the season, games were cancelled by players to protest the shooting of a black man by police in Kenosha, Wisconsin.

As play was about to begin in late July, I decided to keep a blog of my reactions to the season as it unfolded. It was a way to document one aspect of this strange pandemic year while sharing my thoughts about baseball with some fellow fans. My fairly regular entries became an annotated diary of how I experienced the Covid-19 season, a chronological collection of what I noticed, read, and wrote about the game and its players over the three months that baseball was played in 2020.

Not surprisingly, many of the predictions I made along the way about how things were going to unfold turned out to be wrong. But one was not: that even this truncated season would produce its share of great, or at least special, baseball moments. Some of those have been the result of the changes implemented to accommodate the artificial season. Thus, we saw numerous baseball firsts, including a leadoff two-run homer and a complete three-out inning in which only two men came to the plate. But there were also many notable baseball moments that could have happened in any regular season. Two pitchers threw no-hitters, hitters tied or broke home-run records, and Jayson Stark had a wealth of material for his year-end list of strangest plays of the season. Some of the most exciting and interesting players in the game performed up to or above expectations, including: Mookie Betts (who shone as a five-tool player from Opening Day through the last game of the World Series), Juan Soto (who at age 21 led the majors in OPS), and Trevor Bauer (who surprised almost everyone but himself by winning the NL Cy Young Award). And the season concluded with two riveting seven-game League Championship Series, followed by a World Series that ended with three wonderfully entertaining games.

What follows is not a comprehensive account of all the best games played or every significant event over the course of the season. Nor is it a rigorous analytical assessment of which players or teams performed the best. Rather, it is a necessarily idiosyncratic collection of the events that caught my attention, the players that struck me as worth learning more about and writing about in more depth, the games that merited somewhat detailed discussions, the players or games from past seasons I decided to compare to this season's events and players, and the baseball stories I chose to retell.

I grew up in Chicago among a family of Cubs fans and have remained a Cubs fan my entire life. This has meant suffering through decades of many losing seasons, the agony of 1969, and the brutal close calls in 1984 and 2003, before finally getting to bask in the joy of the 2016 championship season. As a result, a number of the entries that follow concern my reactions to the up and down fortunes of the Cubs this season, as well as some more detailed discussions of particular Cubs games or players. But my interests in undertaking this project were broader than just the Cubs. I wanted to write about my relationship to the game as a whole in this particular season, and I have tried to put even these Cubs-specific entries in the context of other teams and players.

Each baseball fan's interaction with the sport is unique. Some follow only their favorite team, or only those teams in the same league. Others keep an eye on the full spectrum of games played across MLB. Some fans are intensely interested in statistics and the performances of individual players, and some embrace the new analytical approach to the game brought about by the rise of sabermetrics. Other fans could hardly care less about advanced statistics beyond those that for generations have been recorded on the backs of baseball cards. I hope that fans of the game, regardless of their particular interests and team loyalties, will find something that resonates, or at least piques their interest, in this account of how one fan experienced a weird but ultimately rewarding baseball season.

PART ONE

The Season

60 Games to Glory

B ASEBALL HAS FACED a variety of external challenges over the last 120 years and has played through them all. It survived two world wars, neither of which cost the sport a single season—nor did the 1918 influenza epidemic that killed 675,000 Americans, the Great Depression, polio and tuberculosis outbreaks, or a World Series fixed by professional gamblers. None of these crises has had as big an impact on games being played as the Covid-19 pandemic, which has brought baseball to its knees. On March 12, MLB shut down every team's spring training camp. Announcement that the start of the season would be postponed at least until the middle of May followed four days later. And now the 2020 season comes down to a 60-game sprint that will unfold, almost certainly, in a bizarrely quiet atmosphere, with no fans in the stadiums where the games are played.

The season's first games will be played on July 23 and the "regular" season will end on September 27. Some players, including a few of the game's best, have opted not to play at all rather than expose themselves and their families to the virus, and no one knows how this socially distanced season will actually play out.

A fair number of baseball fans and commentators have argued that what is about to begin is not a *real* season—that 60 games are not a true test of the best teams. True, this season will not be the usual endurance contest in which some teams surge to the front, only to fall far behind by the end of the year, and others languish in April but emerge as dominant in their divisions by September. It will not be a measure of which team has the depth of talent to survive a 162-game marathon. But the 10k, which covers barely a quarter the distance of a marathon, is nevertheless a staunch test of a distance runner. And the 60-game schedule—two solid months of daily games—will still be a test of baseball excellence.

Those who find 60 games too small a sample size to separate the best teams tend to ignore that baseball's postseason uses an extremely short playoff series to identify its championship team. One-game Wild Card eliminations, five-game divisional playoffs, even the best-of-seven LCS and World Series championships all come down to which team's players produce in a handful of games. Statistically, even the best players can be expected to underperform with some frequency within the constrained timeframes of these series. Most fans acknowledge that luck and timing often have as big a role in determining the winner of the World Series as which is the "better" team. So, too, in this truncated season—more so than over a full 162-game schedule—there will be a heightened element of randomness. Some great players will not perform up to their usual high standards, while some less-than-great players will put up unexpectedly great numbers, and the best team on paper may not even make the postseason.

It will, no doubt, be a different kind of season. Every game will matter more—more than twice as much as a game in an ordinary season. The best players will be under greater pressure to play up to the level expected of them. Managers' decisions will be magnified because of the relative importance of each game. It will not be the leisurely six-month excursion we are used to, where nothing seems really urgent, and all but the most hopeless of seasons have some hope of being salvaged, until the calendar reaches August. This year, teams that endure a long losing streak or have a bad month will not be waiting to catch fire; they will be on life support.

Some baseball records will be irrelevant this year. No batter is going to beat Bonds' record of 73 home runs, or surpass Ichiro's 262 hits, or drive in more runs than Hack Wilson's 191. And many traditional milestones of an outstanding season—for pitchers, 250 strikeouts or 20 wins; for hitters, 100 RBI or 40 home runs—will be out of reach. But other records remain in play. There are enough games for a hitter to break DiMaggio's 56-game hitting streak or be the first to hit five home runs in a game. Some pitcher could surpass Orel Hershiser's 59-inning scoreless streak or be the first to strike out 21 batters in a nine-inning game. Or some unlucky hitter could be the first to make all three outs in an inning. (George Kell of the Boston Red Sox came the closest on June 18, 1953, when he batted three times in the Red Sox half of the seventh inning and made two of their three outs.)

So, as baseball fans we can complain that it isn't a real season because it is different. Or we can view it as what every baseball season is: a daily contest to see which team can rack up more wins than the rest. And in that regard, the fundamental things apply. Good pitching, solid defense, timely hitting and, maybe most importantly this year, unexpected achievements by second-tier players will win games. The teams whose players do more of those things, albeit over a shorter span of games, will come out on top. That is not so "different." And as in every season, each day will provide 15 opportunities for something special, or even unique, to happen.

"Let's Make Some Noise"

W E KNEW THE stadiums were going to be devoid of fans and that watching the games on TV was going to include numerous images of empty seats—empty seats behind home plate as the background of every pitch; thousands of empty seats in plain view as the camera gives us a wide shot toward first base on a ground out; empty seats where home-run balls land in the outfield bleachers.

But I had given less thought to the silence in which the games would be played. I don't know why. I had watched the remotely produced versions of Saturday Night Live and shows hosted by Bill Maher and Jimmy Fallon. The bits on SNL and the usually laugh-inducing monologues by Maher or Fallon were starkly different with the absence of live-audience feedback. The humor just didn't resonate without an audience response. Maher, in subsequent shows, sought to remedy this by having obviously fake laugh tracks inserted and intercutting stock footage of audiences from events decades earlier. The irony helped, but just a little. The laugh-track technique is hardly new. For years, TV sitcoms produced with no live audience used canned laughter to make the shows more entertaining. And as we are frequently reminded, baseball—no matter how much we mythologize or idealize it—is an entertainment business.

MLB did think about the silence and understood that this would magnify the emptiness of the park. They realized that energy emanating from the stands would be a key element missing from baseball of the pandemic—that home team heroics without any vocal fan response would be like a clever joke that elicits no laughter. They also recognized that the ever-present background buzz of the crowd we take for granted as a part of every televised game is an important ingredient of a fan's viewing experience. So they decided to use prerecorded crowd noise in every ballpark where games will be played this season. MLB has stipulated: "All Clubs will use ambient and reactionary background audio to create crowd noise during the 2020 season." This "crowd track" will be audible to the players on the field and to the television audience.

To facilitate this augmented reality, MLB has provided each team with "an array of crowd sounds" and a touchpad device that teams can use to integrate these sounds with the park's audio system. The background sounds and reactions have been derived from a video game, MLB The Show 20, which utilizes original source audio created by MLB from recordings of games. These recordings were "meticulously edited into sound cues used in MLB The Show 20, with a focus on authentically replicating crowd sound and behavior." Teams are not required to use the soundtrack provided by MLB and are free to develop and use their own. Either way, the home team will be in control of managing and operating these imported audible crowd reactions.

Most of the players who have heard the crowd track being used during "summer camp" games have reacted favorably, though some have said the volume was too loud (!). Fan reaction, at least at this point before the start of the season, has been more mixed. In a Yahoo Sports online survey, 58 percent of respondents said they wanted to hear crowd noise on broadcasts of games played in empty stadiums, while 42 percent said they did not.

In a further effort to replicate the reality of fan-filled stadiums for those watching the games on television, MLB has incorporated one more feature. An MLB app, Cheer at the Ballpark, will allow fans watching at home to react in real time and have their reactions translated into the simulated crowd reaction at the ballpark. As described in bleacher-report.com, "The App will keep tabs on the percentage of fans who are cheering for each team and how they are reacting and then relay it to staff inside the stadiums to impact the fake crowd noise."

This raises all sorts of interesting questions. If the Chicago Cubs are playing in Pittsburgh and most of the fans watching the game on TV and logged into the app are Cubs fans, will the piped-in crowd reaction make it sound like a home game for the Cubs, or will the PNC Park sound crew have the ability to override or ignore the input from the app? When the Cardinals are at Wrigley Field on a weekend in August, will the crowd track reflect what it is really like at such a game, where a significant number of fans in the park are Cardinals supporters who have driven up for the games? And when the Cubs play the Brewers in their home opener on July 24, will the "crowd" boo Ryan Braun each time he comes to the plate?

How this piped-in crowd noise is going to work for us as fans remains to be seen. For now, I will leave to philosophers this question: If someone smacks a home run—and the only sound we hear is the recorded cheering of a generic crowd at some baseball game in some ballpark in some prior season—is it real baseball, or a video game?

SHORTLY BEFORE THE first game, Fox announced that on the MLB games it broadcasts, not only will there be crowd noise piped into the park, but there also will be virtual fans digitally placed in the seats. The network will utilize "cutting edge Pixotope software, partnering with Silver Spoon Animation and SMT, to bring a unique experience to baseball fans nationwide." Fox will have the ability to control the attendance at each game it broadcasts, though just how they will make this decision has not been explained. Fox did explain that "fans will dress according to the weather and will show emotion depending on what happens in the game." And, as if this were a good thing, "They could do the wave." A Fox Executive VP emphasized, "We aren't trying to fool anybody. It's not like we are trying to make people feel like there is a crowd there." Oh. Maybe it is a video game, or at least a new virtual reality.

Should We Do This?

B EYOND DEBATING WHETHER this is going to be a "real" season, one worthy of our attention, there is another issue. In a July 21 piece in the *Washington Post*, Dave Sheinin posed the question (and he is far from alone in doing so) whether it really makes sense to bring back not just baseball but all sports in the middle of a global pandemic. Thus, he asked: "We're really going to send our best athletes back onto their fields and courts, in empty stadiums and arenas, despite their own trepidation, sometimes spoken, mostly not?" And we are going to do so when more Americans are infected and hospitalized with Covid-19 than when the season was put on hold in mid-March?

Baseball players themselves have not been unanimous in thinking that the upcoming season is a good idea. Among the more notable players who have not just raised concerns but have chosen not to play at all are: Buster Posey, David Price, Ryan Zimmerman, Mike Leake, Ian Desmond, Nick Markakis, Felix Hernandez, Jordan Hicks, and Michael Kopech. As Buster Posey asked one week before he opted out of the season: "What are we doing?" Other players, while acknowledging the legitimacy of that question, have an answer. The Cubs' Anthony Rizzo summarized his view this way: "We have an opportunity to bring joy to a lot of people that are home through these tough times." Even the upbeat Rizzo was quick to note, though, that "if guys start testing positive left and right and this thing gets out of control," he is confident many players will opt out.

Sean Doolittle, the closer for the Washington Nationals, echoes Sheinin's point about the absurdity of playing while the pandemic rages on, but objects on another level—that America doesn't deserve baseball because we haven't earned it. "We haven't done any of the things that other countries have done to bring sports back. Sports are like the reward of a functioning society." Whether America was a sufficiently "functioning society" to have earned the "reward" of baseball could have been asked numerous times during the history of the sport. Did we deserve baseball during all the years when highly skilled black athletes were denied the ability to play in the major leagues, or during the fifties and sixties when black stars did appear on major-league teams, but in some parts of the country those players could not stay in the same hotels or eat at the same restaurants as their white teammates? Once we start questioning whether, as a society, we are worthy of having sports to entertain us, we are off down a long and murky path.

Sheinin says that athletes being sent onto the field for our entertainment at the risk of contracting Covid-19 are akin to the gladiators of Rome who faced death in the Coliseum in order to entertain the masses. But (as Sheinin recognizes) there is an element of this inherent in most of the sports we watch. Think of Formula One or NASCAR racing, where drivers face a very real risk of a fatal or devastating accident each time they take the track—or football, where players face a likelihood of incurring one or more crippling injuries over their careers, not to mention the risk of traumatic brain injury from repeated cranial impacts. Baseball poses less risk relative to some other sports, but every time a pitcher steps on the mound and delivers a pitch to the plate, the batter risks getting hit in the head with a ball coming at nearly 100 mph. And the pitcher faces the same risk from a line drive coming back at him even faster. Athletes take risks to entertain us. This is nothing new.

Baseball is, to most owners, intended to be a money-making enterprise, and like owners of bars, restaurants and numerous other businesses, its owners want to get back to making money. They are attempting to do it in a way that minimizes the risk to the athletes and the teams' other employees, many of whom also want to return to earning money. Whether it is possible for baseball to do that is an open question, but their attempt does not strike me as less moral than any other business trying to resume operations consistent with whatever rules local government imposes and any guidance on best practices the CDC and other medical experts provide.

If there is a moral problem with the return of baseball, and similarly the NBA, NFL and NCAA football, it is this: these sports all anticipate frequent, rapid-response testing of their athletes during the season. For baseball alone, that will mean tens of thousands of tests for players and staff over the course of the 60-game season. But medical experts tell us we are still far from having the level and speed of testing among the populace at-large that we need to control the virus. How do we justify diverting those limited resources to athletes solely for the sake of our entertainment? If a vaccine suddenly becomes available, it seems unlikely most fans would argue that athletes should be the first to get it so that we can bring back sports.

So, as a fan who very much wants to see baseball again, I think about all these things, and I am conflicted. Regardless of where I come out, though, it appears that baseball will be played, at least for now. Tonight, weather permitting, Gerrit Cole will face off against Max Scherzer in Washington. And Anthony Fauci, the icon of America's effort to control the Covid-19 pandemic, will throw out the first pitch. What could be better entertainment than that?

Opening Day

I HAVE BEEN watching baseball for more than sixty years, and in all that time I do not remember ever looking at the baseball landscape and saying: "I've never seen *anything* like this." But last night, I did. The games were played in empty stadiums with piped in sound, cardboard fans in the seats, managers and umpires wearing masks, and TV announcers calling the action from remote locations around the country. None of us have ever seen anything like this. But strange as all this was, it wasn't the biggest story about these games.

Four years ago, Colin Kaepernick knelt during the national anthem to protest racial inequity in America, and he was publicly ostracized, attacked by the President and blackballed by the NFL. Last night, the pregame ceremony centered on a video montage of players pronouncing the need to speak up about ending racial inequity in America. In each park, players on both teams arrayed along the baselines knelt together before the game, holding a long continuous black ribbon to signify their unity on this issue. A modified MLB logo with BLM below the familiar silhouette was stenciled on the mound, and BLM adorned the side of each base.

In Los Angeles, several Giants players, joined by manager Gabe Kapler, knelt during a rousing gospel version of the anthem. On the Dodger side, all stood except for Mookie Betts, who knelt and bowed his head. Max Muncy and Cody Bellinger, flanking him on either side, each put a hand on one of Mookie's shoulders. Before he rose to his feet, Betts gave each a tap on the back of the calf to show his appreciation. Later, between innings Kapler talked during his dugout interview with the network broadcast crew not about hitting or pitching but about the need to fight systemic racism in America. None of us have ever seen anything like this.

But even with the cardboard fans, fake soundtrack, and social justice motif—once the games started, it still looked remarkably like baseball. Both season openers offered attractive pitching matchups. In Washington, it was Gerrit Cole, newly a Yankee, against the indomitable Max Scherzer. In Los Angeles, HOF-bound Clayton Kershaw was to face off with the always entertaining Johnny Cueto.

In the first game of the night, Cole ended up with the five-inning win, his team leading 4–1 when the skies opened up and rain ended the game in the top of the sixth. Cole pitched the way the Yankees are paying him to do, giving up one run on only one hit through his five innings. Scherzer, who took the loss, was uneven. He looked like the same old Max at times, striking out 11 Yankee hitters, but he also struggled with command, walking four and giving up six hits. The loudest hits were by Giancarlo Stanton, who launched a 460-foot two-run bomb in the first and then drove in another run on a line shot to right. Stanton, who the Yankees acquired (along with the remaining $295 million of his contract) from the Marlins in 2018, played in only 18 games last year. The Yankees are expecting him to have a lot of days like this.

We got an early taste of what may happen to teams' rosters in this season of Covid-19 as Juan Soto, already a star at age 21, was forced to sit out because he tested positive for the virus shortly before the game. The team apparently got a waiver of the Washington, DC rule mandating 14 days of self-quarantine for anyone coming into contact with a person who has the Coronavirus, and no other Nationals sat out. As it was, the Nationals' lineup—with Soto sidelined, Ryan Zimmerman opting out of the season, and Anthony Rendon gone through free agency—looked like a shell of the one that brought them a World Series ring last year.

The second marquee matchup fizzled before it ever got started. Earlier in the day, the Dodgers announced that Kershaw had strained his back in the weight room and would not be able to make the start. Instead, the Dodgers sent 22-year-old Dustin May to the mound to pitch Opening Day. Before this start, May had pitched all of 34 innings in the big leagues. He made a striking figure on the mound, with an effusion of bushy red hair that would make Carrot Top envious pouring out beneath his cap.

Mookie Betts, age 27, came to the plate for the first time as a Dodger one day after signing a 12-year, $365 million contract. He got a nice roar of approval from the sound track when he made a fairly routine catch on his first chance in right field and then thrilled the cardboard crowd when he barely missed getting a force out at second after charging a line drive single and making a quick throw off his back foot. In his fourth plate appearance, he got his first hit as a Dodger on a line drive to left, and he then scored the go-ahead run from third by getting a great jump on a ground ball to second, despite the infield playing in to choke off such a run. In what seems likely to happen a lot this season, the Dodgers, who are loaded, won—and the Giants, who are rebuilding, lost.

Finally, if Covid-19 and BLM were not enough for this strangest of opening days, we learned just before the first game started that the playoffs would be expanded to 16 teams. Only the most incompetent clubs will fail to reach the postseason, and most teams will be in contention until near the end, since you just need to have the eighth best record out of 15. It is entirely possible a team with a losing record will get in. As a result, this now seems likely to be only the second year since divisional play began in 1969 that both the Cubs and the White Sox will reach the postseason in the same year. And so, in this faux season, perhaps Chicago fans will finally get to see a Cubs-Sox World Series. Why not?

Opening Day, Wrigley Field, Etc.

July 25

KYLE HENDRICKS GOT the Opening Day start for the Cubs, and it was a good story. As an excellent feature by Patrick Mooney for *The Athletic* pointed out, Hendricks has been very good for quite a while. He has the sixth-best career ERA in the league among active starters, and he is one of only four starters in baseball to have an ERA under 3.50 in each of the last four seasons (the other three being Kershaw, Scherzer, and Verlander). But, like Rodney Dangerfield, he gets no respect. Although Jacob deGrom has won the last two Cy Young awards on the strength of his superb ERA and sub-1.000 WHIP (despite collecting just 10 and 11 wins in those two seasons), when Hendricks led all major-league pitchers with a 2.13 ERA and posted a 0.979 WHIP (while going 16–8) in 2016, he finished third in the NL Cy Young voting.

Even the Cubs, before this year, have not viewed him as a top-of-the-rotation starter. But he responded to the confidence reflected in the Cubs' decision to have him start this year's opener by pitching a masterpiece. Without ever throwing a pitch over 90 mph, he kept the Brewers hitters off balance all night, mixing his excellent sinker and changeup with effective four-seam fastballs and a newly refined curve. Still, when the broadcast team on ESPN for the late Angels-A's game discussed the day's impressive pitching performances—Jacob deGrom (5 IP, 9 K), Shane Bieber (6 IP, 14 K), Lance Lynn (6 IP, 9 K), and Mike Soroka (6 IP, 0 ER)—they didn't even mention that Hendricks threw a 103-pitch, three-hit, complete game shutout. (There were 11 shutouts, total, thrown by NL pitchers in the 2019 season.)

Apart from the mastery of Hendricks, the star of the show for the Cubs was Anthony Rizzo, whose bad back made it uncertain he would even be able to play in the opener. He walked on four pitches in the first; he graciously offered Orlando Arcia (the only Brewer to reach base against Hendricks) hand sanitizer at first base in the top of the third inning; he was hit (painfully) on the hand in the bottom of the third (to extend his wide lead among active NL players in number of times hit by a pitch); and then he homered in the eighth, pulling an inside pitch down the line in right. The ESPN announcers found it remarkable that Rizzo hit the home run with his back knee on the ground, but it looked pretty familiar to Cubs fans. A classic Rizzo game.

———

ANOTHER FIRST BASEMAN, Joey Votto, is to me one of the most interesting stories in this short season. This was going to be a big year for his legacy. He is 36 and his career stats put him just at the edge of the demanding standard for first basemen to make the Hall of Fame. He had an off year in 2019 after a miserable start and needed a solid 2020 season to cement his HOF case. Now he has only 60 games to do that. Perhaps because the Reds have been a below-.500 team since 2013 and have never advanced past the LDS during his career, Votto is one of the more underappreciated players in the game today. He has won an MVP and five other times finished in the top seven. He has led the league in on-base percentage seven times and has led in OPS twice. As a Cubs fan, I love Anthony Rizzo, a player almost any team would be happy to have as their first baseman. He is a consummate professional who puts up very good numbers every year and has won four gold gloves. But Votto has been significantly better. Rizzo's career slash line (BA, OBP, SLG) is .273/.373/.488. Votto's is .307/.421/.519. Votto went 2–4 in the Reds' opener with a home run. I am pulling for him to have a great 60 games.

One of the more interesting games of the night was the Angels against Oakland. It featured the best player in the game, Mike Trout; the 20th consecutive Opening Day start by the aging Albert Pujols; and the debut of Joe Maddon as manager of the Angels. Not surprisingly, Joe is still Joe—he put the shift on against Matt Olson in the bottom of the second, moving third baseman David Fletcher into short right field but then had Fletcher hustle back across the field to third base when the count went to 2–2.

On the other side, the A's fielded a team with several terrific players many fans have barely heard of because they play the majority of their games when most of the country is getting ready for bed. These include Matt Chapman, who is arguably the best defensive third baseman in the game, Marcus Semien, who finished third in the AL MVP voting in 2019, and Ramon Laureano, who just might have the best arm in baseball. Laureano has only played 171 major-league games before this season but has already recorded 19 outfield assists. And he can hit a little—collecting 24 home runs and 29 doubles in 123 games last season.

The player who gets my second vote for most intriguing story of the year is Shohei Ohtani, who this season will again attempt to be both a run-producing hitter and a regular member of the Angels' starting rotation. Ohtani did not pitch last season, as he recovered from Tommy John surgery. But he did play as DH in 106 games, batting .286 and hitting 18 homers, a power decline from his rookie season numbers. His .880 OPS after two seasons still puts him in the upper echelon of hitters. As a pitcher, he made only 10 starts in 2018 before elbow pain shut him down, but that small sample was impressive: 3.31 ERA and 11 K/9. As Tom Verducci summarized Ohtani's tools based on metrics gathered from Statcast: "Ohtani hits the ball harder than Bryce Harper, runs to first faster than Trea Turner and throws harder than Gerrit Cole." That is quite a skill set.

Ohtani is scheduled to pitch Sunday's game against the A's, and the Angels expect him to pitch once a week for the 60-game season. He is also recovering from knee surgery at the end of last season, so the Angels' current plan is not to have him in the lineup the days before and after he pitches, though Maddon has indicated that may be subject to revision, depending on how Ohtani reacts. But if they stick to the plan, he would only be in the lineup for about half the Angels' games. It promises to be another tantalizingly small sample of just how well Ohtani can do something no player since Babe Ruth has done: be a star hitter and star pitcher at the same time.

Change We Can Believe In?

B ASEBALL FANS, AT least those who have been watch-ing the game for a couple decades or more, no mat-ter their politics, tend to be conservatives when it comes to change in their sport. And with good reason. One of the things that has made baseball great is its relative continuity. MLB is not like the NFL, which seems to revise its rules every other season.

Before this year, there had not been a significant change in the rules governing how baseball is played (as opposed to rules affecting the meta game, such as the video replay rule, or expansion of teams qualifying for the postseason) since adoption of the designated hitter for the AL in 1973. And that is a good thing. It is what allows us, at least somewhat meaningfully, to compare the performance of players from different eras and to see how the game has evolved playing with one stable set of rules. Changes such as the decline of complete games, stolen bases and sacrifice bunts, and the skyrocketing numbers of strikeouts are organic changes that have occurred as a result of evolving performance within the rules, rather than because of rule changes.

This year, MLB has implemented three significant changes to rules governing play of the game: a universal designated hitter rule, a sandlot gimmick to try to resolve extra-inning games more expeditiously, and a new rule requiring relief pitchers to face at least three batters in an inning before being replaced. And as if that were not enough, MLB has revamped the postseason. Those of us who fall into the category of baseball conservatives are going through the baseball equivalent of a cytokine storm—our immune system is going berserk trying to fend off the virus of change that is infecting our game in this pandemic season.

The Universal DH—Apparently embracing Churchill's dictum that one should "never let a good crisis go to waste," MLB has seized on the opportunity of this disrupted season as an excuse to finally slide the designated hitter rule over to the National League. The DH rule remains, in my view, an abomination. Nine players take the field when the opposing team bats, and those nine should bat in order when their team comes to the plate. There is an inexorable symmetry to this. Had Moses brought the rules of baseball down from Mount Sinai, it seems inevitable that this is one of the things that would have been carved on the tablets.

I know the arguments against pitchers batting: they are lousy hitters (almost always the worst in the lineup); they can get injured running the bases; the DH extends the careers of guys who can swing a bat but can't play defense worth a lick; etc. I find none of these justifications convincing. Most (though not all) pitchers are going to be the worst bat in the lineup, but that just makes their less-frequent hits that much more entertaining. Remove from baseball's grand highlight reel the greatest moments by a pitcher at the plate—Tony Cloninger's two grand slams in one game, Kerry Wood's home run in Game 7 of the 2003 NLCS, Bartolo Colon's first career homer at age 43—and the game's history is diminished. And once you say pitchers aren't going to bat, it just means some .220 hitter is now going to be the worst bat in the lineup. Yes, pitchers can pull a hamstring running hard to first base, but so can the star shortstop or right fielder. As part of their training regimen, pitchers run at least as much as position players. The notion that their legs are too fragile to run the bases seems silly. Finally, while I am all in favor of people having jobs, baseball is a game of both hitting and fielding. If your bat doesn't outweigh your poor glove (as, say, Dave Kingman's did), you shouldn't be on a major-league roster, or at least not an every-day player.

The Extra-Inning Rule—The new rule for resolving games that remain tied after nine innings is a classic example of a solution in search of a problem, or at least a bad fit between problem and solution. Few would disagree that baseball has an issue with games being too slow and running too long, but extra-inning games have almost nothing to do with that. Almost half of the extra-inning games that have been played over the past decade have ended in the 10th inning, which is the minimum time it will take to end games under the new rule. And roughly 65 percent of extra-inning games are over by the end of the 11th. It remains to be seen whether the new rule will materially change this percentage. Certainly, the rule makes it easier to score a run, raising the chances from about 27 percent to 61 percent by starting the inning with a man on second base. But that is true for both teams. One thing the new rule will do is give a greater advantage to the home team that can avoid being scored on in the top of the inning.

Managers like the new rule because it eliminates marathon games that can exhaust a team's bullpen. This may be a real problem for a manager when it happens, but those games are so rare (roughly one half of one percent of games played each year go past the 13th inning) that these freak games hardly seem like a justification for adopting a rule so foreign to the game as arbitrarily placing a runner on second base. Others say marathon games result in the unseemly use of position players to pitch. But managers are just as likely to put a position player on the mound in a nine-inning blowout as in a 17-inning battle of attrition.

I am skeptical that the new rule will necessarily result in more exciting baseball. Of the two extra-inning games played so far, one was decided by a walk-off home run (which seems hard to attribute to the magic runner on second) and the other after a run scored on a sacrifice fly in an inning that did not involve a single official at bat (runner placed on second, sacrifice bunt, sacrifice fly, walk, out stealing).

The Three-Batter Rule—Even conservatives can be reasonable, and I am willing to entertain that requiring a relief pitcher to face three batters might not be a bad idea. It is not that there is anything inherently wrong with managers using frequent pitching changes to exploit matchups. But pitching changes are among the least fun things in baseball. The deadening of the game's pace produced by repeated pitching changes can be stultifying to a fan trying to stick it out in late innings of a game already three hours old. And especially this year with the expanded rosters that allow teams to carry a clown car full of relievers, it is not hard to imagine games grinding to an unbearable slog if mangers can bring in a new pitcher three or four times an inning.

The Postseason Picnic—Finally, MLB has revamped the playoff structure by expanding the postseason to include more than half of the teams in each league. This is a change clearly designed to meet a real problem: the owners' and the networks' loss of revenue. Given the proliferation of games the first-round best-of-three series will produce (up to 24 games), this change addresses baseball's need. MLB has tried to avoid having this cheapen the division races within each league (in which the top two teams in each division plus a couple of wild cards get in) by providing that all three games will be played in the park of the team with the better record. Given the lack of hometown fans in the ballparks, whether this will turn out to be a significant advantage will be an interesting experiment—if the season gets that far.

Is This the End?

W E DO NOT know for sure when the Marlins will play baseball again. Or the Phillies, depending on their test results. With the schedules of the Yankees, Orioles and Nationals also disrupted, baseball's 60-game season appears to be hanging by a thread. Those players who have elected to play are expressing increasing concern. Among those who opted out, David Price has been outspoken with "I told you so," while Buster Posey, who asked, "What are we doing?" has been more circumspect. To those who believed the season was a huge mistake all along, this is vindication. To those who believed some baseball was better than no baseball, it is a splash of cold-water reality.

With 15 Marlins players and two coaches testing positive for Covid-19, MLB announced yesterday that all of the Marlins' games through Sunday would be postponed. And the Phillies, who played the Marlins in the season-opening series, will not play again until Friday while its players get tested. The schedule has been rejiggered so that the Marlins' and Phillies' scheduled opponents, the Yankees and Orioles, will now play each other in Baltimore to avoid downtime.

The Nationals, who were to play Miami this weekend, will be idle for those days. How all this will get sorted out before the end of September, assuming no more teams have an outbreak, remains to be seen, but the already dicey season is now teetering on the brink of chaos. Among other things, there is the prospect of the Marlins having to play, once they resume, with a roster of minor leaguers if the team complies with local governments' 14-day quarantine rules. Commissioner Manfred has declared baseball has not yet reached a "nightmare scenario," but nobody is sleeping very well.

And yet, baseball games continue to be played, and stories continue to be written on the field in the same vernacular in which baseball stories have always been written. Shohei Ohtani is hitting .140 and in his one start was charged with five earned runs without recording a single out, resulting in the highly undesirable ERA of infinity. Meanwhile, because almost nothing and no one in baseball is unique, there is another player attempting the Ruthian feat of being a hitting pitcher and a pitching hitter: the Reds' Michael Lorenzen, who has also been testing this dual role on a limited basis for several years. His results have not been outstanding. Appearing almost exclusively as a relief pitcher, his ERA has hovered around 4.00; as a hitter, he has a career batting average of .235 with a total of 11 extra-base hits in 132 at bats over five seasons. His chances of pulling this off seem longer than those of Ohtani.

Elsewhere, in the first meeting between the 2017 World Series contestants since revelation of the Astros' sign-stealing scandal, bad blood between the Dodgers and Astros was quickly evident. Things boiled over in the sixth inning when

Joe Kelly, after throwing ball four behind Alex Bregman and a high, tight pitch to Yuli Guriel, threw a fast ball over Carlos Correa's head, prompting dirty looks and shouts from the Astros' dugout. Order was maintained until Kelly eventually struck Correa out and reportedly punctuated it with a taunt of "Nice swing, bitch." (Kelly later owned up to only the first two-thirds of that utterance.) That led to both benches participating in a decidedly not socially distanced gathering at home plate and produced one of the early season-defining images as Astros' manager Dusty Baker jawed with two members of the umpiring crew, all loudly stating their views through their masks.

On Further Review

I N THE SEVENTH inning of Wednesday night's game between the Cubs and the Reds, the Cubs faced a dire situation: The Reds had two runs already in, the bases loaded, and no outs. Duane Underwood Jr. was brought in from the Cubs bullpen, and under the new rules he would have to face at least three batters unless the inning ended before that. He only had to face one. On a 0–2 count, Shogo Akiyama hit a sharp, low line drive toward third base. Kris Bryant snared the ball just off the dirt, stepped on the bag to double the runner off third, and threw over to Anthony Rizzo, who did the same at first base to complete a triple play. It was a miraculous escape—except that, on further review, it was an illusion. The ball had actually hit the dirt first, and the Cubs had not really gotten three outs. The play stood as called, however, because catch/no catch in the infield is not a reviewable play.

The illusory nature of the Cubs' miraculous triple play struck me as an apt metaphor for the current baseball season. It is, in many respects, a miracle that baseball is being played at all. Given the continued resurgence and spread of the Covid-19 pandemic during July, the notion that MLB could successfully stage a two-month season with games played in 30 different stadiums around the country, with roughly 900 ballplayers and hundreds of coaches and support staff all participating in a nonquarantined manner, seemed a long shot at best. And yet, for several days as the season began to get underway, it looked very much like they were going to pull it off. But now, on further review, it seems like this improbable success may turn out to be an illusion.

The Marlins' situation is obviously the most glaring current problem, with the number of infected players now up to 16—over half their roster. The Phillies, who played the Marlins last weekend, abruptly announced yesterday they were canceling on-field workouts, and MLB today revealed that the Phillies, as a result of two coaches (though, so far, no players) testing positive, will not play again before Monday. And most recently, the Cardinals' scheduled game against Milwaukee tonight has been postponed because two Cardinals players have tested positive for Covid-19. The Marlins and the Phillies now face having more games left to play than there are days before the end of the scheduled season. Several teams currently do not know for certain who they will be playing next week.

MLB is working on ways to deal with these issues, including playing seven-inning doubleheader games to make up for postponements, and is considering the possibility that not all teams will play 60 games, so that postseason qualifiers would be decided by win percentages rather than the traditional won-lost calculus. These measures would compound the other compromises the league has already made to play this unique season, including: playing games in empty stadiums with fake sound effects and fans, adjusting the rosters and roster-move rules, adopting a universal DH, and concocting an artificial form of play for extra-inning games.

Initially, I was not convinced that it was a mistake to try to play a season. Yes, baseball is "just" a form of entertainment and therefore can be considered expendable. But it also plays an important role in the lives of countless Americans for whom this diversion, normally a regular part of their summer activities, can provide a needed psychological boost at a time when many are coping with the stresses occasioned by the pandemic and its consequences. In part, I believe that is why baseball has always been played, even in times of dire national emergency or turmoil. (Think of the memorable Yankee Stadium game shortly after the 9/11 attack.) Moreover, like a wide range of businesses that have been savaged by the country's efforts to control the pandemic, MLB employs many people beyond the most visible highly compensated players, who depend on the game for their livelihoods.

I was not (and still am not) sympathetic to the arguments that it was pointless to play because this was not a real season. Many other businesses and forms of entertainment have adapted and innovated in ways that leave them a far cry from their familiar identities but nevertheless allow them to continue serving their customers. Restaurants, for example, which have built reputations and successful businesses on presenting food in a particular way, have been reduced to serving diners via delivery service or curbside pickup. This doesn't replicate the full restaurant experience their loyal clienteles have enjoyed for years, but people adapt and derive some pleasure from what remains.

So, too, with baseball; the owners, players and broadcasters have sought a way to carry on not as the same enterprise we have known for decades but as *something* that retains the identity and offers the rewards of the game. No one is expected to confuse the 60-game season with the traditional baseball seasons that have been part of our lives every summer for as long as we can remember, any more than we confuse the meals we take home in aluminum containers from a favorite Italian restaurant with those we used to enjoy in a leisurely two-hour meal amidst the enlivening bustle of apron-clad waiters and other diners. Some attribute baseball's insistence on attempting to play a "season" to hubris and greed, and surely that is part of it. But the effort also reflects what many Americans desire: to bring back, even in limited form, the way of life to which they are accustomed and without which their lives feel diminished.

It is, however, increasingly hard to avoid joining the chorus who say that it was a mistake for baseball to have even attempted to hold this season. Given that MLB's schedule has the teams traveling from city to city and staying in hotels or at home with their families, it will not be surprising if more players or coaches test positive in the coming weeks and more teams face Covid-disrupted schedules. It now appears that it was a mistake for MLB to insist that all teams (except where prohibited by law) play games in their home ballparks, even though the stands will be empty and the games could instead be played at a central location where isolation of the players is at least theoretically possible. The decision to let the players live at home while playing in their hometowns and not be quarantined when on the road is reaping what now seem like highly predictable consequences.

It may well be that playing all games in a centralized location and securing all the players within a "bubble" (as the NBA is doing) for two months was simply not feasible. If that is the case, I am coming to the conclusion that baseball probably should not have resumed at all—not because 60 games is not a "real" season, but because the risk to the health of the players, coaches, and other team employees was simply beyond reasonable control. That MLB is now engaged in further daily contortions of the game to vindicate its decision to play is making that conclusion harder to resist. And the league's uneven reaction to the risks of the virus (such as letting the Marlins-Phillies game go forward last Sunday) is making it harder to take seriously Commissioner Manfred's incantations that player health and safety is of "paramount importance."

Nevertheless, until it does implode and they pull the plug, I continue to follow the games being played. I am glad to have a Cubs game every day. I look at the box scores and game stories each morning to see what kind of baseball heroics or absurdities may have occurred. I continue to look forward to the next bit of Javy Baez fielding magic, or dominant pitching performance by Max Scherzer, or electric hitting display by Vlad Jr., or phantom triple play, or even a leadoff two-run homer—or any of the other stories that make baseball so interesting.

Extra Innings Redux

A COUPLE DAYS ago, I said my piece on the new extra-inning rule, which allows the batter who made last out in the preceding inning to appear, magically, on second base to start the next inning. I thought I was done with that, but now there is a minor groundswell of enthusiasm for this new rule by some writers whose work I enjoy and respect. And the reasons offered just don't make a lot of sense.

Take Jayson Stark, a wonderful baseball writer who has a deep affection for all that is special about baseball. He published a piece in *The Athletic* on July 30 with the tag line (borrowed from another writer): "The extra-inning rule is half-court baseball—and it's awesome." His arguments in support of this gushing enthusiasm, in my view, reside on a spectrum from specious to nonsensical. Here are a few:

- In the seven extra-inning games played so far under the new rule, there has not been a proliferation of sacrifice bunts. Stark assembles data, analyzes it, does projections, and concludes the sacrifice bunt will not be used that much more often than its current state of disuse under the regular rules of baseball.

He makes it sound like we are talking about the eradication of polio or smallpox: Thank God it will not come back! Is this an affirmative reason to love the new rule—that it likely will not lead to resurgence of a discredited strategy that has fallen into disuse?

- The new rule, he says, will require managers to take strategy to a heretofore unknown level of depth and complexity in deciding what to do in an inning beginning with a runner on second base and no one out. Managers will now have "a billion things to think about" when a game goes into extra innings. Teams' analytics departments, he reports, have gone into overdrive, crunching "more numbers than the IRS." So, before 2020, what did a manager do if his first hitter doubled to lead off the 10th inning—scratch his head, grab his crotch, and flip a coin on what to do next? Or what if, as apparently can now wondrously happen under the new rule, a runner got to third with one out in the top of the 11th? Had no team ever thought what to do in this situation (or any of the others that can arise in extra innings) before the new ghost-runner rule?

- The new rule, he argues, will also open up wonderful new strategic options for managers, such as the "five-man infield"—bringing in an outfielder with the winning run on third and fewer than two outs in the bottom of the inning. Haven't managers been doing that for years? One strategy that would be new is the intentional strikeout. Say, you have speedster Billy Hamilton batting in the bottom of the ninth with two outs and nobody on. Rather than have Hamilton try to reach, perhaps steal a base, and score on a hit by the next batter to win the game right there, Stark suggests a savvy manager could have Hamilton intentionally strike out so that he would start the bottom of the 10th inning placed on second base. Even assuming this may be a statistically sound strategy, is this really something we would view as baseball progress?

- Looking back to the experience of one minor league where this rule has already been used on a trial basis, he cites a "classic" 15-inning game between the Inland Empire 66ers and the Modesto Nuts in 2019. Put aside that the rationale for the new rule is to eliminate these tiresome "marathon" games. Stark argues this game was special not just for its length but because it featured a stretch in which the two teams scored in nine consecutive half innings, something he says has never happened in a regular MLB extra-inning game (six being the record). Again, can it really be a justification for rewriting the rules that, once in a blue moon, out of the relatively small number of extra-inning games played every year, the teams might score in not just six but now nine consecutive half innings?

- After making the case that the new rule will not cause teams to utilize the tedious strategy of bunting the magic runner over to third base, Stark argues that the rule will have the benefit of bringing back the disappearing "wheel play," a strategy for defending a sacrifice bunt with a man on second where, among other things, the third baseman charges and the shortstop rotates over to cover the bag at third. So, there won't be a lot of dreaded sacrifice bunts in extra innings but enough apparently to bring back the beloved wheel play.

- Finally, Stark posits that this new rule creates the opportunity for some team to sign Usain Bolt (or someone like him), whose sole job would be to pinch run as the guy placed on second in extra innings. It would, he suggests, be like the good old days of the 1970s when Oakland owner Charley Finley signed track star Herb Washington to be a designated runner. Washington once scored 33 runs in a season without ever having a plate appearance. Yes, we have all been longing for the return of that specialist's role. (Just think what the next Eddie Gaedel could do as an extra-inning pinch hitter when the bases are loaded.)

Stark offers other justifications for the greatness of the new rule, but none of them make any more sense.

Sam Miller, writing for ESPN.com, made similar arguments in a July 31 piece entitled "MLB's new extra-inning rule is here and—surprise—it's glorious." Here is a partial list of things that happened in just the first five extra-inning games that he says have produced "the most exciting baseball played this week":

- a walk-off grand slam
- a 3–5 (first to third) fielder's choice to cut down the go-ahead run
- a rookie doubling home a run on the first pitch of his big-league career

- a sacrifice bunt
- a runner caught stealing third
- Pete Alonso coming to the plate as the tying run with two men on
- a pickle play involving Shohei Ohtani as the runner
- two hit batsmen
- two wild pitches
- a walk-off triple
- multiple close plays at the plate

With the exception of perhaps the sacrifice bunt and the two hit batsmen, these are all occurrences that rightfully appear on a list of things that make baseball fun to watch.

But it is hard to make the case (and Miller does not really try to do so) that these exciting things happened *because of* the new rule. Rather, he writes that, contrary to his expectations and those of other baseball pundits, the new rule has not made extra-inning baseball duller. He has been pleasantly surprised that the same variety of strategy and action that occurs in "regular" baseball has occurred under the modified rule. While this may be laudable, it is again not much of an affirmative case for changing the rule in the first place.

The history of baseball, both during the regular season and the postseason, is filled with memorable extra-inning games. They have produced walk-off home runs, close plays at the plate, three more perfect innings by Harvey Haddix, unexpected heroics, and every other kind of play that makes baseball rewarding to watch. Perhaps the new rule has not so far curtailed the range of events that have unfolded for the last 120 years of playing extra innings by the same rules as the first nine. But what has it added? None of the occurrences Miller finds so satisfying and interesting required starting the inning with a runner placed on second base.

In the end, Miller applauds what he sees as the upside of the new rule: that it gets games to end sooner. "It's fun watching these games end," he says. And he tries to make a case that knowing the game will end soon allows managers to employ some different strategies. But as noted in an earlier post, over the past decade most extra-inning games already ended in the 10th or 11th innings. Miller decries those very rare marathon games when he goes to sleep before the conclusion (even while acknowledging that they can be "truly memorable" games). This seems like a very thin reed on which to rest the case for inventing an entirely new rule.

Speeding Things Up:
A Modest Proposal

August 2

IT HAS OCCURRED to me that maybe I have been too hasty in my judgment on the recent extra-inning rule change. I wrote that it was no good argument for the new rule that it had simply produced the same kinds of varied baseball occurrences as the "old" rules. After this past weekend's extra-inning games, there was another rush of enthusiasm from both managers and sportswriters for the excitement engendered by the new rule. And in part that was because it had generated something extremely rare in baseball: things we have never seen before.

Among all the bizarre or outstanding things that can happen during a game, it is almost never the case that that thing has not happened before in the history of baseball. But under the new extra-inning rule, in the span of barely 10 days, we have seen numerous such "firsts." These have included: the first-ever leadoff two-run homer, the first-ever leadoff double play (and a rare 7–5 one at that), and the first-ever situation in which the hitter scheduled to bat third in the inning never got a chance to come to the plate because three outs had already been recorded before it was his turn.

The possibilities now begin to seem endless. Given the rationales driving support for the rule—resolving games faster, introducing new and exciting strategies, and achieving never-before-seen baseball occurrences—here are some further suggestions to improve the game:

- Since a game tied going into the ninth inning presents exactly the same situation and strategic possibilities as the 10th inning, why not extend the extra-inning rule to the ninth inning as well. Start each half of the ninth with a man on second, and extra innings can more often be avoided altogether.

- Although the strategic considerations and game-ending possibilities may not be the same, given the added excitement and variety the rule appears to be producing, why not go a step further and adopt the ghost-runner rule for all innings of the game? Wouldn't it be more exciting if every inning started with a man on second?

- And while we're at it, why limit the rule to starting the inning with a man on second? Instead, how about a rule that allows the home team manager to designate before each inning how it will begin: nobody on, runner on second, bases loaded, etc. The rule would apply in both halves of the inning, so it would be fair. And think of how much more variety there would be from inning to inning.

The possibilities posed by expanding and augmenting the man-on-second rule also ought to open the door to considering other ways to improve the game by making it go faster. Here are a few that seem worthy of serious consideration:

- MLB has already implemented the seven-inning game for doubleheaders. Why stop there? Everybody says baseball games, now averaging over three hours, take too long (even if they don't go into extra innings). Why not make seven innings the new official length of a game? This would have one immediate and obvious advantage: restoring the complete game as a real (rather than highly remote) possibility for starting pitchers. Sure, it would mean that no one is ever going to break Barry Bonds' single-season home run record (or for that matter ever again match Ruth's), but that seems like a small price to pay. And for those nostalgic for three-hour-plus games, don't worry—Boston Red Sox seven-inning games will still take that long.

- Baseball has already adopted a sandlot gimmick with the runner-on-second rule, so why not implement another one that has stood the test of time: four fouls and you're out. Does anyone really want to watch 14-pitch at bats? Either put the ball in play, draw a walk, strike out, or sit down and give someone else a shot.

- Along similar lines, the four balls/three strikes framework is starting to feel a little stale. If you want better tempo, a three-and-two model would seem more suitable to the needs of a game that is falling out of touch with the pulse of the times.

- Finally, is it really necessary to have three outs per inning? Once we have gotten past the psychological barrier of abandoning 27 outs per game (see seven-inning rule above), it seems like only a stubborn adherence to a historical relic argues for continuing to require three outs before moving on to the next half inning.

If baseball is ever going to try to reinvent itself to attract and hold today's short-attention-span sports fans, maybe all the strangeness engendered by this pandemic is just what it needs to finally do so.

Reason for Hope

I DON'T REALLY believe in curses or jinxes, so I write this without concern about the consequences: It looks, at least today, like MLB may actually draw back from the abyss and manage to pull off this season. The Marlins and Phillies are playing again, and the Cardinals, who are scheduled to resume play this weekend against the Cubs, seem to have gotten their outbreak under control. With the aid of the seven-inning doubleheader and some scheduling sleight of hand, they may actually find a way to get their 60 games played.

More importantly, MLB has demonstrated a heightened level of urgency by issuing new, stricter guidelines in an effort to avoid a repeat of the Marlins' and Cardinals' situations. It remains to be seen whether the players will be rattled enough to take the mandate seriously for another 50 days and whether that will be enough if they do. The whole thing could still easily fall apart, but there is some reason for optimism that the 60-game season, and the postseason that would give some stamp of significance, will play out.

And since I don't believe in jinxes, I will say that the Cubs are off to their best start since 1969 (a year that still brings a sour taste to the mouth of any Cubs fan old enough to remember the team's late-season swoon to the Miracle Mets). It is a small sample size, but it is also one-fifth of their season. Given the low threshold for making the post-season, it is hardly surprising that Baseball-Reference.com gives them a greater than 97 percent to do so. (Of course, last year they had a 75 percent chance to make the playoffs with only 12 games left to play and still found a way to miss out.)

The Cubs early success can be attributed to a number of factors, two of which are reminiscent of the championship 2016 season. First, and most important, their starting pitching has been terrific. In 12 starts, every member of the rotation has a WHIP under 1.000. Yu Darvish, though he was roughed up early in one start, has shown the same command he had during the second half of last season, giving up only two walks in his three starts, while fanning 16. Tyler Chatwood, who makes his third start tonight, has struck out 19 and walked only four batters. That is a far cry from his disastrous 2018 season when he led the league in walks, averaging nearly one per inning pitched, and had more walks than strikeouts. Hendricks, while having one bad start, has been strong in the other two; Jon Lester has, at least in two starts, found something in his mechanics to compensate for one more birthday; and Alec Mills has been very good, as he was at the end of last season.

The second thing that in these early games has looked like 2016 has been the Cubs' defense, which last year had regressed from outstanding to borderline awful. Javy Baez has, not surprisingly, made some brilliant plays, including adding one more to his unique highlight reel of great tags at second base. Kris Bryant has made big plays at third, Albert Almora made the catch of the week in the Cubs' first series when he flashed his new red glove high against the green ivy to snare a drive just under the basket, and David Bote has made a number of outstanding plays at both third and second. As was the case with their starting pitching, the Cubs' defense in 2016 was the best in the league.

There are some obvious questions. Will the starters keep up anything like their performance out of the gate? And will the relief corps come together? Craig Kimbrel is still a faint hope as closer, and while Jeremy Jeffress has been excellent so far, it remains to be seen whether he has actually regained the form he showed in his outstanding years with Milwaukee. On the other hand, the hitting, which currently is tops in the league in OPS, seems more likely to continue at a high level, barring injuries or a Covid-19 outbreak. So, on balance, it would seem that there is reason to hope the Cubs can chase down the first asterisked championship in MLB history.

Keys to Success

THE NEW YORK Yankees and Chicago Cubs have gotten off to strong starts in this 60-game season. The Cubs' early success is attributable to a number of factors: some outstanding pitching from every member of the starting rotation; excellent defense; timely hitting; enthusiastic and vocal support from the dugout to replace, at least in part, the feedback from real home fans in the seats; and the apparent positive impact of new manager David Ross. For the Yankees, their early success has reflected production from their two big bats, Stanton and Judge, plus 26 total home runs in their first 15 games. But, as Marc Craig and Patrick Mooney discussed in an excellent piece Friday in *The Athletic*, there is one more factor, unique to this season, that is at work for the Yankees and Cubs: their ability to deal effectively, at least so far, with the threat of Covid-19.

As Craig and Mooney explain, both teams have been aggressive not only in implementing the MLB protocols but also toward facilitating their players' compliance with them. The ability to avoid the kind of outbreaks that have struck the Marlins', Phillies', and Cardinals' rosters may be a key to success over the 60-game season. Even if an outbreak does not decimate a lineup, as happened with the Marlins, it can (just like the ever-present risk of injury) deprive a team of a couple key players to quarantine in a season where even a few games without them can matter. And it can force teams into playing punishing schedules to complete the 60-game sprint. That is the case with the Cardinals, who after being forced to cancel this weekend's series against the Cubs now face the prospect of playing 55 games in 49 days.

The Cubs have taken a number of steps to try to avoid an outbreak in their ranks. The team has booked hotels with large outdoor areas to serve as isolated open-air lounges where players can hang out and still remain socially distanced. These hotels provide three meals a day for players on the road to eliminate their need to go off the hotel grounds for food. The team has also added buses running every 20 minutes between the hotels and ballpark so players can avoid crowding together on arrival and departure trips. In short, team management has not simply relied on players' personal sense of responsibility or self-interest but has also committed financial resources to minimize the risk of having the virus infiltrate the team and its staff.

The Yankees similarly have committed substantial resources to protecting their players. Among other things, they have secured large hotel ballrooms and convention spaces in which player workouts, trainer sessions, and video reviews prepare players for games—all activities that normally would take place in more confined spaces at the ballpark. And they have made these spaces into entertainment-based lounges to keep their players off the streets and prevent them from gathering together in small hotel rooms.

While the Cubs have not been perfect—postgame victory congratulations still sometimes involve skin-to-skin contact—as a team they appear to understand that, as Theo Epstein explained, "Everyone is at the mercy of the least responsible person." In part, that buy-in has come from the personal way the team faced the issue before the season began. David Ross, a rookie manager who came in carrying instant credibility with at least a good number of the team's veterans, tied the importance of compliance to members of the team. Craig Kimbrel has a young daughter at home with a heart defect that has required multiple surgeries—and two team members, Jon Lester and Anthony Rizzo, are cancer survivors. Tommy Hottovy, the Cubs' pitching coach, is only 39, but described to the team his grueling 30-day fight to recover when he contracted the virus. As Jason Kipnis, with three close friends who have suffered through Covid-19, noted, "you don't want to be the one that screws this up." Yu Darvish, a key to the Cubs pitching, said he would have gone home if he had not been satisfied the team and his teammates were treating the Covid-19 issue seriously—and he has stuck around.

The Cubs and Yankees have been two of the teams most aggressive early in the season in seeking to avoid outbreaks, but they are obviously not the only ones that have avoided that fate so far. Still, at least one unnamed player on another team that has yet to have anyone test positive has expressed frustration that his organization has not been willing to take the steps teams like the Cubs and Yankees have taken to protect their players. And players on the Cubs, such as Ian Happ, have been open in stating their appreciation for the commitment the team's senior management and owners have made to protect the players.

Whether the Cubs' diligence has been the difference between them and teams like the Cardinals and the Marlins, or just good luck, is unknowable at this point. As Theo Epstein noted, every person he knows outside baseball who has contracted the virus "has done everything right." And so, it remains to be seen whether the Cubs' efforts, along with those of other teams under MLB's newer, more stringent guidelines, can get them through at the two-month season and possibly another month of postseason play without having an outbreak that forces them to suspend play and put some of their players on the shelf. It may end up being a lesson for all of us in just what it takes to avoid both contracting the Coronavirus and being a person who transmits it to others in the community.

Forfeit?

A S BASEBALL AGAIN teeters on the brink, with MLB announcing the cancellation of the Cardinals' upcoming series with the Pirates this week, questions about what is going to happen with all the unplayed games, assuming the season continues to its late-September conclusion, become more acute. The Cardinals, if they resume play after the Pirates series, will face the prospect of playing 55 games in 46 days. In other words, they will have to play 46 consecutive days, with doubleheaders on nine of those days. Even with the new seven-inning doubleheader rule, that is a lot of baseball in a month and a half. Apart from the burden it would place on the Cardinals players, it is also a burden on their opponents, who will have to endure the scheduling contortions necessary to make up the games they have missed with the Cardinals.

This raises the question (beyond the more obvious one about whether MLB should complete the season at all) of why these games should be made up. Rule 7.03(b) of the Official Rules of Major League Baseball provides: "A game shall be forfeited to the opposing team when a team is unable or refuses to place nine players on the field." The Cardinals, for 10 days, have been unable to field a team against their opponents. One possible way to deal with this situation (and those of the games the Marlins were unable to play) is that they should be forfeited, and the opponents credited with wins for the missed games. Would this be fair?

Consider what would happen if a team bus broke down on the way to the ballpark (say, from Chicago to Milwaukee) and the team failed to secure alternative transportation to arrive in time to begin play at a reasonable hour. Would it be unfair to have them forfeit the game? Maybe not. What if their charter flight could not take off for a day because of a hurricane, and they missed a game? This feels like a different situation, one in which the teams and MLB would agree to make the game up on another day. And that is in fact what has happened in such situations. Or what if a team suffers a tragedy in its family? On June 22, 2002, the Cubs were scheduled to play the St. Louis Cardinals in Wrigley Field. That day, after the Cardinals had arrived at the ballpark, the team learned that pitcher Darryl Kyle had been found dead in his hotel room. Not surprisingly, the stunned and grieving Cardinals were not willing to take the field that afternoon. The game was postponed and rescheduled, by agreement, for another date later in the season. I do not recall ever hearing a suggestion that the Cardinals should have forfeited the game.

Forfeits are rare. Only five major-league games have been forfeited since 1970, and four were the result of riotous behavior by home team fans (including Cleveland's ill-advised 10-cent beer night and Disco Demolition Night in Chicago's Comiskey Park). Only one game has been forfeited because the team failed to play, a game between Baltimore and Toronto in September 1977 when Earl Weaver ordered his players off the field in the fifth inning because he deemed the playing conditions unsafe. The umpires disagreed and ordered the game forfeited after Weaver refused to bring his team back on the field.

But this year is different. Whether it would be unfair to have teams forfeit games they were unable to play because one or more of their players had contracted Covid-19 depends on whether one thinks that the kinds of outbreaks that have occurred on the Cardinals and Marlins are the fault of the players and/or the teams' management by failing to adhere to the MLB protocols designed to prevent this from happening. The anecdotal reports vary on whether the Marlins' and Cardinals' outbreaks can be attributed to bar-hopping and other similarly risky behavior by members of the teams. As Theo Epstein recently observed, you can do everything right and still manage to contract the virus. If it really was just bad luck that a pandemic rendered them unable to play, why should the Cardinals, Marlins and any other team who suffer a similar fate be punished by forfeiting the games they were unable to play?

One argument for what could be deemed a harsh application of Rule 7.03(b) is that it would create the strongest possible incentive for teams to be scrupulous in adhering to MLB protocols and to protect themselves and their teammates from the virus. (Under this theory, it would not be reasonable to have the Phillies forfeit the games they were unable to play because they had to quarantine for several days while being tested after being exposed to the Marlins in the season-opening series.) In a season in which the inherent "unfairness" of the game is magnified by the risk of having star players go on the IL with Covid-19 or opt out of the season entirely, the notion of what is fair becomes skewed. Is it fair to require other teams to play ridiculous schedules so Covid-affected teams can make up missed games? Or is it fair to allow the Cardinals to qualify for the playoffs based on their winning percentage if they only play 54 games? The season is a mess, and somebody's ox is getting gored by the consequences of teams whose players have been infected with Covid-19. Rather than make things even more absurd, why not treat Covid cancellations as one more bad bounce and move on?

Then Play On

O N July 25, the third day of the 2020 baseball season, Peter Green died. He was one of the founding members and the artistic force behind Fleetwood Mac before they became the Stevie Nicks-fronted pop phenomenon that sold millions of records starting in 1975. After graduating from the John Mayall school of blues, Green was the lead guitarist and song writer that made Fleetwood Mac one of the best British blues bands of the late sixties. He may not have had the flash of Jeff Beck or the unique skills of Jimi Hendrix, but his admirers ranged from Eric Clapton and Jimmy Page to B. B. King. He left the band in 1970 after excessive LSD use and a religious conversion led him to renounce all pecuniary gain from music, and he was later diagnosed with schizophrenia. He continued to play sporadically after that, but it was never the same. Listening again to the Fleetwood Mac albums released in 1968 and 1969 in the days after that announcement, it was hard not to wish there had been more.

So, too, with baseball in this compressed and truncated season; following the stories each day that are managing to drown out the Covid-19 bad news, it is impossible not to wish for more. For most teams the season is already at least one third over, and there are so many good stories that will feel incomplete.

It is frustrating that we will not see more this year of Mike Trout, the best player in the game. Trout turned 29 this month and, while still in the prime of his career, is also statistically past the age at which major leaguers reach peak performance. Trout is off to a great start this year and shows no signs of slowing down, but playing now in his tenth season in the majors, it is hard not to think that the remaining years at his current level of greatness may be countable on one hand. Albert Pujols, whose hitting numbers for his first 10 years surpass even those of Trout, began to decline in his age-31 season.

Of course, before we become too wistful about Trout losing the better part of one prime-of-career season to the Covid-19 pandemic, we should not forget the three years Ted Williams missed to serve in World War II—his age-24, -25 and -26 seasons. Williams had led the league in OPS for the two years before his military service, and he did so for four straight years after his three-year stint as a naval aviator. And as a reminder of how great a hitter Williams was, in every one of those six years, his OPS was higher than that of Trout's best season. Comparisons to Williams aside, Trout has already put a Hall of Fame career in the books, having won three MVP Awards, compiled a career OPS of 1.001 (best among all active players), and contributed WAR of 73.2 in just nine seasons. We want to see as much of this great player in his prime as we can.

It is frustrating that a handful of players looking to put the final touches on thier Hall of Fame resumes will not have a full opportunity to do so. Some active players, of course, would have been locks to make the Hall even if not a single game had been played this year. This is plainly true for Albert Pujols and Miguel Cabrera. For Pujols, the only remaining suspense is how high he will finish on the all-time home run list, as he is about to pass Willie Mays for fifth place.

Three current pitchers likewise have almost certainly earned their spot: Clayton Kershaw, whose 2.44 ERA over 12 seasons, three Cy Young Awards, and an MVP make a compelling case even if he never pitched another inning; Justin Verlander, with 3,000 strikeouts, 225 wins, two Cy Young Awards and six more top-five finishes; and Max Scherzer. Scherzer is a classic case of a pitcher who didn't hit his stride until his late 20s. Over the last seven years, starting with his age-28 season, Scherzer has led the league in wins four times, led in strikeouts three times, had WHIP below 1.000 four times, won three Cy Young Awards, tossed two no-hitters, and had a 20-strikeout game.

This season is probably also not material to the HOF chances of Yadier Molina. He is in his 17th major-league season, all behind the plate, and he has nothing left to prove as a great defensive catcher. He has made nine All-Star teams, won nine Gold Gloves, and has a respectable .281 career batting average. While maybe not as obvious a candidate as Pujols or Cabrera, there is likely nothing another full season in the twilight of his career could do to change anyone's mind.

But there are several players for whom another strong season could be what they need to write their ticket to Cooperstown, and it would have been fun watching them try to do so. One of these is Joey Votto, who has been a great hitter for many years, but is not generally viewed as an obvious Hall of Fame candidate. In an era that values on-base percentage more than ever before, Votto has excelled in that category, holding the highest OBP (.427) of any active major leaguer. His 284 career home runs and 954 career RBI are not impressive for a first baseman, but his career OPS of .939 is the 28th best of all time, and he is one of only 23 players ever to have a career slash line of .300/.400/.500+.

Another player who may be in this twilight category is Zack Greinke. Now in his 17th season, he began the year with a career ERA of 3.35 and is second (to Justin Verlander) among active pitchers in career wins. He is also tied with Verlander for highest career WAR (71) among active pitchers and is behind only Albert Pujols and Mike Trout among all active players.* While he may not have the gaudy numbers of pitchers like Jacob deGrom, Kershaw,

---

* Wins above replacement (WAR) has become one of the more prominent of the new metrics we have received from the world of sabermetrics. WAR purports to tell us how many more games a team won as a result of a particular player's contributions, as compared to a hypothetical "replacement" player, generally defined as one barely good enough to climb from the minor leagues onto a major league roster. Many elements of a player's performance go into calculating his WAR, and there is no consensus on exactly how those inputs should be weighted. There are two widely recognized sources for WAR, each based on a slightly different formula: Baseball-Reference and FanGraphs. Throughout this book, all references to WAR are to the metric as calculated by Baseball-Reference.

or Scherzer, he has been a consistently excellent pitcher for many seasons, with a couple of great ones, and could use one more good year to fill out his resume.

There are other veteran players who may not be burnishing Hall of Fame careers but are nevertheless also good stories. For example, it is frustrating that we will not get to see if Nelson Cruz could have matched David Ortiz's final season in Boston for best performance in recent history by a hitter at age 40. Cruz broke into the majors in 2005 at age 24. He didn't play regularly until the 2009 season, in which he turned 29. In his first five years as a regular player, Cruz averaged 27 home runs, hitting more than 30 just once. In his next six seasons, through 2019, he averaged 41 home runs, the number he hit last year, and more than 100 RBI. Last season, he posted a career-high 1.031 OPS. And he has been durable, averaging more than 550 AB over those six seasons. Cruz turned 40 before baseball resumed in late July, and he is the heart of the Twins batting order. In his first 23 games, he is hitting .354 with eight home runs, but we will have to wait until next year to see if he can produce at an exceptional level for a full season as an age forty-something hitter.

Finally, it is frustrating not to see what some of baseball's great young stars would do for a full season. The list of outstanding players under age 23 includes: Juan Soto, Ronald Acuna, Fernando Tatis, Vladimir Gurrero Jr., and Bo Bichette.

- Juan Soto, who is 21, hit 34 home runs and drove in 110 last season for Washington as a 20-year-old playing in his second season with the Nationals. Soto's advanced metrics (OPS+ and wRC+) for his first two years put him among the top four players in history through their age-20 seasons. He missed the beginning of this season after being diagnosed with Covid-19, but in his first 10 games is batting .405 with six home runs, including a 463-foot bomb against the Mets last week. Everyone who sees him play echoes the view that he is something special.

- Ronald Acuna, a year older than Soto, is also already in his third big-league season playing outfield for the Atlanta Braves. He was Rookie of the Year as a 20-year-old in 2018, and then last year hit 41 home runs, stole 37 bases, drove in 101, and scored a league-high 127 runs. He is off to a slow start this year (.258 with four home runs), but it is hard to believe he will not be a star in this league for many years.

- Fernando Tatis, who is 21, batted .317, hit 22 home runs, and was credited with 4.1 WAR in just 84 games as a rookie shortstop for the Padres last year. Through 24 games this year he is batting .304 and is leading the majors in home runs and RBI. Despite his obvious raw talent, Tatis has many skeptics who focus principally on his shaky defense. Tatis has great range and a canon arm but has shown a tendency to have mental lapses on easy plays (especially coming in on the ball) and has had problems controlling his throws to first. Of the 18 errors he made last season, 14 were throwing errors. (He is, in many respects, a better-hitting version of the young Shawon Dunston who debuted with the Chicago Cubs in 1985 with a similar set of tools, and similar issues.) Nevertheless, even a long FanGraphs piece making the case for his defensive liabilities concludes that Tatis "is one of the most exciting players in baseball," who unquestionably "is capable of greatness."

- Vladimir Guerrero Jr., also just 21, came into the league last year with the Toronto Blue Jays as the most highly touted prospect in years. (Like his Toronto teammate Cavan Biggio, Guerrero is the son of a Hall of Famer, and along with Bo Bichette forms part of a trio of young second generation players starting for Toronto.) Guerrero, who had destroyed minor-league pitching since starting in the Blue Jays' farm system at age 17, did not live up to the great expectations for him as a 20-year-old rookie last season. He hit a respectable, but ordinary, .272 with 15 home runs in 123 games, and his defense was, at best, shaky. And so far in this shortened season he is hitting .242 with just three home runs. We may have to wait until next year to see if Guerrero can become the breakout star that so many have predicted, or will be yet another can't-miss prospect who fails to deliver at the big-league level.

- Bo Bichette, at age 22, has already been dismissed as an overachiever, based on the expectations formed during his brief minor-league career and what the analytics geeks like to call "peripherals," advanced metrics that suggest his short-term major-league numbers may not be sustainable. Last year, he hit .311 with 11 home runs in 40 games as a 21-year-old rookie shortstop with Toronto. In 17 games so far this season, he is hitting .361 with five home runs. He has just been sidelined with a knee contusion, which means his 2020 season may not provide a larger sample than his relatively short debut last year.

It is too bad we will not get to see how these five budding stars would have continued to develop this year over the course of a full 162-game season.

In addition to these precocious 21- and 22-year-olds, there is a crop of exciting young talent just a year older, including: Rafael Devers, Glyber Torres, Yordan Alvarez, Eloy Jimenez, and Ozzie Albies.

- Rafael Devers began playing third base for the Red Sox at age 20. After struggling for his first two years, he had a breakout season last year, hitting .311 with 32 home runs, and leading the league in total bases. Although he is at best an adequate third baseman and does not take a lot of walks, he is a player who has the bat skills to turn into a star.

- Glyber Torres was one of the prize prospects in the Chicago Cubs organization until the Cubs traded him to the Yankees to obtain the services of Aroldis Chapman for the final three months of their 2016 World Series season. The Yankees brought him up in 2018 at age 21. Although he has been a below-average fielder at both shortstop and second, his .274 batting average and 62 home runs in his first two seasons have made him an integral part of the Yankees lineup.

- Yordan Alvarez played only 87 games for the Houston Astros last season, but it was enough to win him the

Rookie of the Year award. In just over half a season, he hit 27 home runs, drove in 78, and posted an eye-popping .313/.412/.655 slash line. It is unclear whether he has a place to play in the field, but it does seem clear that his bat will be in someone's lineup for years to come.

- Eloy Jimenez, like Alvarez, has shown a great bat, but little ability to play the field. Unlike Alvarez, he has insisted he does not want to DH, or even be removed for a defensive substitution late in the game. So Sox fans have had to endure watching Jimenez struggle to corral balls in left field, including badly misplaying one high fly down the line into an inside-the-park home run this season. But in his rookie season for the Sox last year, Jimenez hit 31 home runs in 122 games, and he already has hit seven in 20 games this year.
- Ozzie Albies has played in the shadow of Ronald Acuna but has gotten better each year since the Braves made him their second baseman at age 20. Last season, he batted .295, hit 24 home runs, and drove in 86. And unlike each of the other four 23-year-olds above, he is an above-average fielder. But because he is a free swinger and doesn't have the raw power of the other players on this list, some have questioned whether he has reached his ceiling as a player.

Given the limitations each of these players has shown, in addition to their obvious talents, it seems likely only two, or at most three, will become long-term star players. Which those will be is just one more story that will have to wait a little longer to be fully written.

Bote Does It Again

D AVID BOTE HAS been a role player for the Chicago Cubs since he came up as an unheralded 25-year-old rookie in 2018. But that year, on the night of August 12, he hit one of the most memorable home runs in Wrigley Field history. The game, against the Washington Nationals, had been a wonderful pitchers' duel for seven innings between Max Scherzer and Cole Hamels, but the Cubs were trailing the Nats 3–0 with two outs in the bottom of the ninth when Bote came to the plate as a pinch hitter with the bases loaded. Down to his last strike, on a 2–2 count, Bote drove a knee-high fastball deep over the wall in straight away center field for a walk-off grand slam. The crowd of 36,000, most of whom were still there, erupted in a roar of ecstasy as Bote flew around the bases.

Tonight, just over two years later, Bote came to the plate as a pinch hitter in the sixth inning (of a seven-inning game) in the nightcap of a doubleheader with the St. Louis Cardinals. The Cubs had already lost the first game and were staring at their fifth straight loss trailing the Cards in this game 4–2. The Cardinals, who had missed 12 of their scheduled games to a Covid-19 outbreak on the team, had been a speck in the Cubs' rearview mirror just a week earlier as the Cubs sprinted to a 13–3 start, while the Cards remained stuck at 2–3. But if the Cardinals won this game, they would pull within a game and a half of the Cubs.

The Cubs had managed only one hit in the game so far— their first run scoring on three walks and a passed ball. But they now had runners on first and third with two outs and one run in on Willson Contreras's double. On a 1–0 count, Bote got a fastball down the middle, just over knee high, and again drove it deep into the batter's eye in straight away center field. It was not as dramatic as the walk-off slam two years earlier, and there were no fans in the seats cheering wildly as he circled the bases this time, but it gave the Cubs the lead in a game they needed to win, and it added to the legend of David Bote in Chicago.

Unwritten Rules

T HE COMMON LAW has been developing since . . . well, since long before I was born. So, too, have the unwritten rules of baseball—the sport's common law. None of those rules has ever quite been etched in stone. Is it or is it not permissible to try to bunt for a hit in the ninth inning of a no-hitter? Many players (and fans) might say that violates the unwritten rules, but by no means would all agree. There is probably more agreement that it is unseemly to steal late in a 10–0 blowout. But even on that point, there are some who insist that as long as the opposing team is still trying to win, the game is on and the goal is to score more runs to ensure victory. And, like the common law generally, baseball's code is constantly evolving. The current penchant for bat flips on prodigious home runs, for example, appears to have all but overruled the settled rule against showing up opposing pitchers.

The most unusual situations may prompt the most esoteric debates. In August 1978, Pete Rose had extended his consecutive game hitting streak to 44 but was hitless in the ninth inning when he faced Atlanta closer Gene Garber.

Rose took issue with Garber throwing him an off-speed pitch out of the zone on a 2–2 count, which Rose chased for strike three. Rose complained that Garber had treated the at bat as if it were the seventh game of the World Series. Garber took it as a compliment, saying, "That's how I try to pitch every time I'm in a game." On this one, Rose may have been in a small minority in complaining about a violation of the unwritten rules.

Young players, particularly in today's game, seem to have the most problems with baseball's common law code of conduct. Such was the case last night when 21-year-old Fernando Tatis Jr. came to the plate in the top of the eighth inning with the bases loaded and his team ahead 10–3. Tatis had already hit a three-run homer in his last at bat. This time, on a 3–0 count, he crushed a ball to the opposite field for a grand slam. The first pitch to Manny Machado, the next Padres hitter, sailed behind his head. The message was clear: Tatis had violated baseball's code by swinging away 3–0 with his team holding a late seven-run lead.

Based on my admittedly imperfect knowledge of the unwritten rules, I would not have thought this an obvious violation, especially because the Padres bullpen has been among the worst in baseball and has already squandered several big leads this year. Rangers manager Chris Woodward saw things differently, but also recognized that the unwritten rules continue to be in flux: "You're up seven runs in the eighth inning; it's typically not a good time to swing 3–0. It's kind of the way we were all raised in the game. But, like I said, the norms are being challenged on a daily basis—so, just because I don't like it doesn't mean it's not right."

Padres manager Jayce Tingler was even more ambiguous in his comments. He said he was going to talk to Tatis because he had either missed or disregarded the third base coach's take sign on the 3–0 count. Whether Tingler had called for Tatis to take the 3–0 pitch out of deference to an unwritten rule, or because he hoped to get a free run forced in if the pitcher threw another one out of the zone, he did not elaborate.

————

IN MY FIRST post on this 2020 season blog, I wrote that despite the obvious shortcomings of a 60-game season, which have now been compounded by an artificial rule altering play in extra innings and seven-inning games in doubleheaders, baseball would still be worth watching because it would present multiple opportunities every day for something special to happen. And that has certainly proven to be the case in numerous ways, some unique to this Covid-19 season. Last night, it was the performance of Fernando Tatis Jr., who homered twice and drove in seven runs to take the major-league lead in both of those categories.

But what has become the obsession of the baseball world today is not Tatis's great day at the plate; rather, it is the controversy over whether he should have hit his second home run, an eighth inning grand slam, at all. Since I posted the note above this morning, I have been reading the tidal wave of Twitter comments and other online posts debating whether Tatis violated one of baseball's unwritten rules for swinging at a 3–0 pitch (and swinging hard) with his team holding a seven-run lead. The comments have come from baseball writers like Joe Posnanski and Jeff Passan, to Hall of Famer Johnny Bench, to pseudonymous posters claiming to be former major leaguers, to scores of ordinary fans. It is as much traffic as I have seen on almost any issue so far this season. And these comments cover the full spectrum from: "Tatis was clearly, obviously wrong" to "Are you kidding me?"

Here is Posnanski for the Tatis side: "I didn't realize that there are unwritten mercy rules embedded in the game and breaking those is widely viewed as the baseball version of a capital offense. I didn't realize that baseball treasures its wink-wink, nudge-nudge understandings more than it does the awesome thrill of watching Fernando Tatis swing the bat." And Johnny Bench, from a hitter's perspective: "So you take a pitch . . . now you're 3–1. Then the pitcher comes back with a great setup pitch . . . 3–2. Now you're ready to groundout into a double play. Everybody should hit 3–0." And finally, this anonymous baseball historian: "The Rangers beat a team 30–3 once. And they are the ones complaining?"

On the other side of the debate are comments like this, all generally linking unwritten rules to the glory of the game: "Why are people dismissing guys who think Tatis should take 3–0 up 7 runs late as Old Heads? Respect for the game, team & opponent is what makes baseball great." And this, making the respect point even more personal: "If you played the game, you would understand the ultimate prize is to win like a gentleman." And this: "The unwritten rules are what made the game fun." Past tense.

I am in the camp that Tatis had every right to swing away if he hadn't been disregarding the take sign given by his coach. (Whether it was dopey to give that take sign is a separate issue.) But I think the bigger take-away from this is that what makes baseball great (well, one of the things) is that baseball fans can have these debates. And to those who might think the analogy to the common law is inapt because those uncodified rules are at least memorialized in judicial opinions, law treatises, and the like—while baseball's "unwritten" rules are not—see: Jason Turbow, *The Baseball Codes: Beanballs, Sign Stealing, and Bench-Clearing Brawls—The Unwritten Rules of America's Pastime*; or *Paul Dickson, The Unwritten Rules of Baseball: The Etiquette, Conventional Wisdom, and Axiomatic Codes of Our National Pastime.*

Redemption?

A NOTHER BIG WIN for the Cubs last night. After losing a two-run lead, they scored two runs in their final turn to bat—in the top of the seventh inning. It was their last chance to bat because this was the second game of a doubleheader, and thus was a seven-inning game under the Covid-year rules. And the Cubs were batting in the top of the seventh, even though the game was in Wrigley Field, because the teams were making up a game that should have been (but never would be) played in St. Louis. For the second time in this series of five games in three days, the Cubs were fighting to avoid a doubleheader sweep. And for the second time, David Bote came off the bench to deliver a pinch hit to put the Cubs ahead. Two nights earlier, it was a three-run homer; tonight, it was a line drive single to center with the bases loaded. And then Craig Kimbrel came on to pitch the bottom of the seventh with the Cubs up 4–2.

The last time Kimbrel faced the St. Louis Cardinals, he was the locomotive in a train wreck. In 2019, the Cubs lost four straight one-run games to the Cardinals in Wrigley Field in late September to kill their chance to play in the postseason. In the first game of that series, after the Cubs had tied the game with three runs in the bottom of the ninth, Kimbrel came on to pitch the top of the tenth. He had been, at best, uneven since the Cubs signed him as a free agent in June, but Joe Maddon still had enough faith in him to send him out with one job: keep the game even so the Cubs could win it in their half of the tenth. After striking out Dexter Fowler, he gave up a first-pitch home run to Matt Carpenter, which was enough to beat the Cubs. Two days later, the Cubs had again fought back in a wild seesaw game to take an 8–7 lead. Kimbrel came in to save the game in the ninth inning. The first two pitches he threw, to Yadier Molina and Paul DeJong, left the yard and the Cubs suffered a devastating 9–8 loss.

Cubs fans can certainly be forgiven for thinking the signing of Kimbrel to a three-year deal was a mistake. He was not good last year, and his last two appearances were disastrous. It is easy to forget that after the 2018 season Kimbrel was on many people's lists of active players destined for the Hall of Fame. For nearly a decade, he had been the best closer in baseball, and he is the current leader among active pitchers in career saves. His numbers over those years were outstanding. During his first nine seasons, appearing in 542 games, Kimbrel had an ERA of 2.09, averaged 14.8 strikeouts per nine innings, and had a WHIP of 0.950. His career save percentage, including his rough 2019 season with the Cubs, is 90 percent. Mariano Rivera, the greatest closer of all time, had a career save percentage of 89.

Of course, not every player with a Hall of Fame resume continues to perform at that level his whole career (see Albert Pujols). But when the Cubs signed Kimbrel, he was only 31 years old. The hope, certainly within Cubs management and with less resolve among Cubs fans, was that Kimbrel would bounce back this year.

But Kimbrel's early outings in 2020 were a continuation of the horrific end to his season last year. In his first outing, on July 27, he came in with the Cubs holding an 8–5 lead in the ninth. He walked four batters, hit another, and threw a wild pitch—recording just one out before being removed. His next appearance was not much better. Coming in with the Cubs holding a comfortable 6–1 lead, he gave up home runs to the first two batters he faced in the ninth. On August 4 he came in with the Cubs holding a three-run lead but yielded a single and double to two of the first three hitters he faced (both of whom eventually scored) before being pulled. His ERA at that point stood at 32.40. To make matters worse, after he was removed from those games the TV cameras sadistically held long shots of his pained face in the dugout, while the commentators speculated about what had happened to him.

Lately, though, Kimbrel has shown signs of turning the corner. In his next appearance, on August 14 with the Cubs trailing the Brewers by a run, he pitched a scoreless ninth, yielding just a walk while striking out two Milwaukee hitters. Two days later, again coming in with the Cubs trailing, he pitched a 1-2-3 eighth, again with two punchouts. And last night, David Ross gave him the chance to close a key game. Although he hit Tommy Edman with a sharply breaking inside curve ball, Kimbrel struck out the side, ending the game with a perfectly located fastball on the inside corner that Kolten Wong took for strike three. And equally important, Kimbrel showed the velocity that had been lacking in his prior poor outings. His fastball routinely came in at 97 and touched 99 on at least one occasion. It may be too soon to declare the resurrection of Craig Kimbrel, but there is at least reason for hope.

Baseball Firsts

O NE OF THE great things about baseball is having something happen that has never happened before over the hundreds of thousands of games that have been played in the game's long history. This year has been filled with such events that have resulted from the Covid-season rules changes. These include:

- the first leadoff double play;
- the first leadoff two-run home run;
- the first inside the park leadoff two-run homer;
- the first leadoff sacrifice fly;
- the first loss attributed to a pitcher who came in at the start of an inning and allowed no one to reach base;
- the first walk-off hit in the bottom of the eighth inning;
- the first number three hitter in an inning who didn't get to bat because three outs were made before it was his turn.

Some avid followers of the game, such as the great baseball scribe Jayson Stark, love these things. Stark is a chronicler of baseball oddities, so one can hardly blame him. But these firsts seem cheap to me. While amused, I am not impressed by these events any more than I am by whoever was the first person to be in the starting lineup, play the entire game, but never take the field to play a position. This also happened because of a rule-change gimmick (adoption of the DH), not some unique twist in the fabric of baseball.

There have been a series of baseball firsts that could only have happened this year, but they are not the result of changes to the rules of the game. These are the firsts resulting directly from the reality that baseball is being played in the midst of an infectious disease pandemic. Thus, we are witnessing for the first time an entire season played without a single paying fan in attendance. (The 1918 baseball season was played despite the influenza pandemic that was raging in America that year, until it was cut a month short to support the war effort. But until that happened, fans continued to attend the games.) We have seen twice, likely for the first time, an active roster player ejected from a game for heckling the umpire while sitting in the seats normally occupied by paying customers. We have seen games postponed because members of one team needed to be quarantined after they were exposed to teammates with Covid-19. These "firsts" we hope will simply become part of the lore of the strange Year of Covid.

Apart from firsts attributable to the new rules and the constraints imposed by the Covid-19 pandemic, there has been at least one legitimate baseball first this year. On August 20, Eric Hosmer hit a fifth inning grand slam to put the San

Diego Padres ahead of Texas 5–2. It was the fourth consecutive game in which the Padres had hit a grand slam (by
four different Padres hitters)—the first time in major-league
history that has happened. And, while I am not sure the
records exist to support this, I believe we also saw another
first in baseball history two nights earlier in a game between
the same two teams. In the second inning, with dead-pull
hitter Joey Gallo at the plate, Padres third baseman Manny
Machado was shifted into the hole on the right side. Gallo
lifted a high fly down the right field line, and fairly deep.
Machado took off immediately and after covering 100 feet
made the catch running with his back to the infield in foul
territory just short of the right field warning track—though
the ball was just fair where he almost nonchalantly reached
back to grab it. It is a remarkable play to watch from any
of the several camera angles that captured it. And it is hard
to imagine any other third baseman has made such a catch.

There was a great opportunity last weekend for another
first. On August 16, against the St. Louis Cardinals, the
White Sox hit four consecutive home runs in the fifth inning.
It was the 10th time this had ever been done, but the first
time it had happened with all four home runs coming off a
pitcher, the unfortunate Roel Ramirez, who was throwing
his first inning in the major leagues. Welcome to the show,
Roel. After Yoan Moncada, Yasmani Grandal, Jose Abreu,
and Eloy Jimenez had already gone deep and Ramirez had
departed, the next batter was Edwin Encarnacion, who has
418 career home runs. So, the history-making fifth straight
was definitely in play. Alas, Encarnacion struck out on three
pitches.

I am still hoping this may be the year we see one of baseball's young stars become the first player to hit five home runs in a game or, better yet, have someone become the first to make all three outs in an inning. There is still over half the season left to play. So these firsts remain possible.

The Short Run

A PIECE BY Mike Petriello on MLB.com yesterday focuses on the terrific "all world" numbers Bryce Harper is putting up so far this season. Indeed, through Sunday, Harper leads the National League in OPS (1.119) and trails only the apparently ageless Nelson Cruz for the major-league lead. Harper's current slash line is a very impressive .320/.453/.667. If he could sustain these numbers, they would surpass those of his historic 2015 season in which he was the unanimous MVP choice in the NL and be much better than his very good, but not outstanding, 2019 season. The thrust of Petriello's piece is devoted to addressing the question: What is different for Harper this year?

Petriello is a conspicuous member of the expanding group of baseball writers who discuss the game through the lens of the latest analytical tools. Two things in particular struck me as interesting in his analysis of the possible answers to the Harper question. Could it be, he asks, that Harper has just been very lucky in this short expanse of barely 100 plate appearances? No, he says, because his batting average on balls in play is not in the top 30 in base-ball, and his .338 batting average "is mirrored nicely by his .327 expected average." Both of these observations piqued my interest.

One of the statistical averages that has remained rela-tively constant over the last 100 years of baseball (in con-trast to things that have either fluctuated dramatically or moved inexorably in one direction—like complete games, home runs, strikeouts, batting average, and stolen bases) has been the MLB batting average on balls in play, or BABIP. This statistic reflects the percentage of times a hitter reaches base in at bats that do not result in a strikeout, walk, or home run. While there have been brief periods of wider fluctuations, over the last 100 years BABIP has generally hovered consistently between .290 and .300. And this has remained the case despite advances in the equipment used by fielders to catch the ball, greater numbers of excellent defenders in the game, stronger and faster batters, dramat-ically increased use of defensive shifts, and periods of rela-tive domination by pitchers or hitters.

BABIP featured prominently in a key sabermetric insight nearly 20 years ago when Voros McCracken published an article on January 23, 2001 in *Baseball Prospectus* entitled "Pitching and Defense: How Much Control Do Hurlers Have?" McCracken concluded, after studying years' worth of pitching data, was that "there is little if any difference among major-league pitchers in their ability to prevent hits on balls hit in the field of play." He based this conclusion on his observation that opposing hitters' batting average on balls put in play against a pitcher did not closely correlate to his ERA in a given season. From this, he concluded that

ERA does not provide the truest picture of a pitcher's skill because the number of earned runs allowed by a pitcher over the course of a season inevitably is affected in significant measure by both the strength of the defense behind him and luck. McCracken proposed, and other analysts who have studied the data now generally agree, that the better measure of pitching prowess is one that isolates those things over which the pitcher has the most control: strikeouts, walks, and home runs.

Is the same thing true of hitters? If a hitter has a year in which he hits .320 with a batting average on balls in play of .350, should we chalk this up to him having an exceptionally lucky season and expect reversion to the mean next season? Not necessarily. While pitchers may be relatively indistinguishable in their ability to control the number of balls in play that result in hits, that does not mean that all hitters are equally likely to reach on such balls. To be sure, all hitters benefit from luck—from bloops, dribblers down the third base line and seeing-eye 12-hoppers that turn into hits. But balls that are hit hard and hit on a line have a better chance of getting past infielders, getting down in the outfield, and bouncing off outfield walls. Thus, the best hitters in baseball—those who hit the ball harder and squarer more consistently—tend to have, over their careers, BABIP well above the MLB average. Among active players with at least 2,000 plate appearances over the past decade, three of the players with the highest career BABIP are Christian Yelich, Joey Votto, and Mike Trout.

So why did Petrielllo note that Harper's BABIP was not among the league leaders? Because over a short period of time, luck plays a bigger role, and a high BABIP can make a hitter look better than he is if a number of weakly hit balls drop in or find holes in the infield—just as a hitter who is consistently hitting the ball hard can still have a low average during a period in which everything he hits is at someone. So the point with Harper is that, because his BABIP is not out of line, his outstanding month at the plate cannot be explained by a lot of lucky hits.

What about his "expected average," a term of more recent vintage? With the advent of Statcast, which tracks the exit velocity and trajectory of every ball hit in a major-league game, analysts now have a new statistic to evaluate hitters: expected batting average (xBA). Data comprehensively compiled by Statcast beginning in the 2017 season can calculate how often a ball hit with a particular exit velocity and launch angle can be expected to result in a hit. Expected batting average is the percentage of times a hitter would be expected to reach (also taking into account his actual strikeout rate) given the exit velocity and launch angle with which he puts balls in play. Among other things, xBA can quantify a factor baseball fans have understood instinctively for decades: that, at least in the short run, "hard luck" .220 hitters are a real thing, and so are .300 hitters who may be more lucky than good.

Expected batting average can be a useful tool for evaluating young players who make a splash (or don't) in limited plate appearances. For instance, Milwaukee's Keston Hiura batted .303 in 348 plate appearances as a rookie last year, but his xBA was only .264. This year, so far, he is hitting .240 on an xBA of .214. By contrast, the Cubs' Nico Hoerner, who came up late last year and is getting spot duty this season, has a batting average of .250 in his 144 plate appearances. But his xBA is .298, based in part on his being in the 80th percentile in hard-hit balls, 93rd percentile in strikeout percentage, and 92nd percentile in speed. These metrics suggest Hoerner deserves a chance to play more regularly.

Petriello's point on Harper's xBA is that his batting average aligns pretty closely with how well he is hitting the ball. Again, this suggests Harper is not getting a lot of lucky hits on poor contact. But hitting the ball solidly is not, Petriello notes, the explanation for why Harper's numbers so far this year are much better than last year. In fact, he hit the ball hard more often and hit fewer ground balls last year than he has so far this season. So why is Harper off to such a great start?

The explanation: strikeouts. Last year, although he hit the ball hard consistently and his BABIP was .313, Harper's xBA was only .277 (and he actually batted .260) because he struck out in 26 percent of his plate appearances. This year, his strikeout percentage has dropped to 15. To see how big a difference this can make, go back to BABIP. Among the top 10 in this category over the past decade are DJ LeMahieu and the recently retired Austin Jackson. Both players averaged about 10 home runs a year over that period. Although Jackson had the higher BABIP (.355 vs. .344), Le Mahieu's batting average was 26 points higher (.302 vs. .276). The difference: Jackson struck out 25 percent of the time, while LeMahieu did so only 15 percent of the time. Jackson was a little more likely to reach when he put the ball in play, but LeMahieu made a lot fewer outs.

Not so many years ago, a respected baseball writer dismissed strikeouts as a "meaningless statistic," which to me seems like a strange statement to make. Given the historical average of hitters reaching base roughly 30 percent of the time when they put the ball in play, versus less than 1 percent when they strike out, strikeouts are significantly less productive at bats when measured by the outs they generate. Pitchers who strike out a higher percentage of hitters (assuming a similar rate of home runs yielded) have a big advantage by limiting the number of times a ball put in play can result in something other than an out.

In today's game, though, the emphasis increasingly is on the "three true outcomes"—home runs, strikeouts, and walks. For hitters who can consistently bang a lot of home runs, especially if they also work deep counts and draw a lot of walks, teams are willing to accept 150 strikeouts or more over the course of the season. The theory is that the extra runs generated by free swingers' long balls outweigh all the outs they produce. And striking out, even with men on base, no longer carries much stigma. Contact is a devalued commodity, at least until a team starts an inning with men on second and third and watches them die there after three consecutive strikeouts.

This is, for better or worse, the team the Chicago Cubs have built. So far this year, three hitters in the heart of their batting order—Baez, Schwarber, and Contreras—are striking out at least 32 percent of the time, with Bryant not far behind at 28 percent. Meanwhile, those four are batting .200, .230, .215, and .177. Compounding this, they have hit a total of only 12 home runs, which is same number the White Sox hit in their recent three-game series against the Cubs. And with the exception of Contreras (.259), their expected batting averages—.230, .216, .204—show these

Cubs hitters are not hitting the ball much better than their averages indicate. Thus, they are generating all the costs, but few of the benefits, of swinging for the fences.

The reality is that, over the course of a 162-game season, or even a 60-game season, Bryce Harper is not likely to sustain a slash line of .320/.453/.667. As Petriello notes, Harper has had better stretches over the same number of plate appearances in seven prior seasons, only one of which ended with a slash line like his current one. Similarly, Baez and Bryant are unlikely to slash .200/.250/.350 and .177/.271/.323 over 60 games. But this year, the short run matters more than ever. The Cubs have managed to get out front with a combination of very good starting pitching, excellent defense, and production from the bottom of the batting order. But unless the premier players start hitting the ball hard, their postseason could end up being cut even shorter than the regular season.

Firsts (Again)

A WEEK AGO, the White Sox had the chance to become the first team ever to have five batters hit home runs in five consecutive at bats. The Sox missed that opportunity when Edwin Encarnacion struck out after four of his teammates had gone deep. But less than a week later, the Sox again had an opportunity to make history when Jose Abreu homered in his last three at bats against the Cubs on Saturday night and again in his first at bat off the nearly unhittable Yu Darvish on Sunday afternoon. Abreu, who was clearly dialed in, came to the plate in the fourth with a chance to be the first player in MLB history to homer in five straight plate appearances. Darvish retired him on a ground ball up the middle, however, and that first will have to wait.

That same day, there was a play in the game between Oakland and the Los Angeles Angels that may or may not have been an MLB first, but certainly seems like it could have been. Tommy LaStella led off the third for the Angels with a single and Mike Trout followed with a looper to center. The second baseman and shortstop both sprinted out in pursuit, and center fielder Ramon Laureano, after taking one step back, charged the ball hard and had enough of a chance to catch it that LaStella had to pause halfway to second. When Laureano realized he could not catch it, he slid and snagged the ball cleanly on one hop off his left hip. Executing a perfect pop-up slide, he released the ball with a short arm throw to second before he had even fully reached his feet. The throw, however, was not to either the second baseman or the shortstop, both of whom were out in center field, or to the third baseman, who was covering the bag at third, but to pitcher Frankie Montas who'd had the presence of mind to sprint from the mound to second base. The throw just beat LaStella for a highly unusual (and perhaps unique) 8–1 force out.

Heyward Speaks

O N A WEDNESDAY in the fall of 2016, Jason Heyward was the speaker in what must be the most famous team meeting in Chicago Cubs history. That night, during the 17-minute rain delay between the ninth and tenth innings of the seventh game of the World Series, Heyward spoke to rally a team that had just lost a lead late in that game and now faced a sudden-death finish in the quest to win their first World Series in 108 years. Baseball historians can debate whether it was Heyward's speech to his teammates, Ben Zobrist's perfectly placed late-swing double to the opposite field, or Carl Edwards Jr. and Mike Montgomery conquering the pressure of the moment to secure the final three outs in the bottom of the tenth that was most responsible for the Cubs' win when play resumed. But one thing was perfectly clear afterward: the respect Cubs players had for Jason Heyward.

At the beginning of the 2016 season, Heyward signed a long-term $184 million contract with the Cubs. By many measures, he has not lived up to the expectations on which that contract was based. Over his first four seasons with the Cubs, Heyward has batted around .255, averaged just 12 home runs, and has never posted an OPS above .800. He has, however, continued to play rock solid defense in right field, winning the Gold Glove at that position in 2016 and 2017. During those four years, in which Heyward has struggled at the plate, he has consistently been a positive influence in the clubhouse, not just working relentlessly to improve his hitting, but also being a quietly professional role model to the younger members of the team.

The World Series rain-delay speech became part of Cubs lore, but remarks Heyward made to the team last night may have been even more significant. Days earlier, a black man, Jacob Blake, had been shot seven times by a white police officer in Kenosha, Wisconsin. The Milwaukee Bucks announced earlier in the day that they were going to boycott their scheduled NBA playoff game Wednesday night, and three MLB games were postponed that night due to player protests. Shortly before the scheduled start of the Cubs game against the Tigers in Detroit, Heyward spoke to his teammates and told them he "couldn't go out there and play tonight, not with what's happening." He went on to say: "I can't tell you what's going to happen tomorrow. I can't tell you what's going to happen the next day. But tonight, I need to be a part of what was going on in my community."

As reported by Patrick Mooney in *The Athletic,* Heyward explained, "I strongly believe that I couldn't tell them to not go out there and play the game because I barely know how to handle this." Instead, he told his teammates he would welcome their support if they decided they did not want to play, but also made it clear they should not feel like they were leaving him behind if they did. In fact, he encouraged them to play, saying: "We still have a season going on. We're still trying to accomplish something as a family. I feel your support. I'm going to support you. And that's that." The rest of the Cubs decided to play, and Heyward sat in the Cubs dugout, in uniform, during the game.

Since the beginning of this season, members of the Cubs and other MLB teams, like athletes in other professional sports, have shed their typical above-the-fray detachment from events going on in society around them. In that respect, among the several others that make this year unique, this has been a baseball season unlike any other. Opening Day of the season in late July was marked by various displays of support for action to address racial inequity in America. Heyward was instrumental in the Cubs' decision, as a team, about how they chose to express their views. At the time, responding to the suggestion that he and other athletes should stick to sports, Heyward responded: "I wish I could stick to sports."

While many fans and baseball writers have applauded these demonstrations by professional athletes—whether it is players kneeling before games, or wearing indicia of support for the BLM movement on their uniforms, or speaking out in the media—others have castigated the players for doing this and vowed never again to watch the sport whose athletes have seriously offended them. Some, including our president, have chastised the players for not knowing their place as entertainers who have no business expressing views on issues like racial inequity or police brutality, and have said they should be shunned for committing the sin of "virtue signaling" or being anti-American.

On "Bloody Sunday" in March 1965, John Lewis and hundreds of other civil rights activists were attacked by police as they attempted to march across the Edmund Pettus Bridge in Selma, Alabama, on their way to Montgomery in support of black voter registration. It is interesting to imagine what the reaction would have been if players like Willie Mays, Hank Aaron, Ernie Banks, Frank Robinson, and Bob Gibson had taken a stand then—if they had refused to play on Opening Day of the 1965 season, or publicly spoken out in support of the marchers in Alabama. And what if their white teammates, or at least some of them, had stood in solidarity with these black players? Would it have changed, even slightly, the arc of the civil rights movement and hastened the end of Jim Crow, or would an irate fan base have drummed them out of the sport? We don't know, but it would certainly have focused attention on what was occurring in the American South at the hands of elected officials and members of law enforcement, and it would have made it harder for citizens around the country to remain oblivious to what was going on.

No fair-minded person—at least none with his eyes open to the world around him—can deny that that racial inequity and injustice continues to exist in this country. Many who might otherwise care simply choose to pretend it does not exist, for then there is no reason to demand change. Not so many years earlier, millions of Americans who might personally have rejected the depredations of Jim Crow that persisted for 100 years after passage of the Fourteenth Amendment closed their eyes to its existence, and by doing so allowed it to continue. Today's athletes are saying they will not be complicit in that silent acquiescence.

When he addressed the team during their pregame meeting last night, Heyward explained his position succinctly: "It's time for us to stand up and be a part of the cause and not just sweep it under the rug." Although a relatively small percentage of MLB players are African American, teams are standing up together as seven more games have been cancelled tonight, not because of the pandemic but because players, black and white, want to show solidarity with the cause of racial justice. I have been critical of many things that have happened in baseball this year, including questioning the decision to play at all. But the actions by players during the last 24 hours make me proud to be a baseball fan.

Back

Y ESTERDAY, WHILE DRIVING back from an errand that had made me risk Covid-19 exposure once again, I looked at the license plate of the car in front of me: PRFCT 27. The reference was unmistakable. But whose car was it? Was Mark Beuhrle in my neighborhood? The plate was on a Prius, so probably not. But Phil Humber, maybe. (As Chicago baseball fans know, both Beuhrle and Humber threw perfect games this century for the Chicago White Sox. Buehrle's, his second career no-hitter, was the capstone of an outstanding career; Humber's perfect game was the only complete game he threw in a 16-win major-league career.) In any event, it seemed like an omen, or a prod to get back to writing about baseball, which had been pushed aside by other bits of life's business.

Strange as it seems to write this, the season is winding down. The Cubs (26–19 going into tonight) have only 15 games left. Although they have played under .500 ball since their hot 17–3 start, they have a three-game lead over the Cardinals, who are in the midst of playing 23 games in the next 16 days to try to finish their full schedule. Who knows what will happen? The Cubs almost certainly have enough cushion to qualify for the 16-team postseason tournament, whether or not they secure "home field advantage" in the opening best-of-three series.

The White Sox, surprisingly to many, currently have a better record than the Cubs (at 27–16) and lead their division by a game over Minnesota. They are similarly a virtual lock for the postseason. So the possibility of the strangest-of-strange—a Cubs-Sox World Series—continues to exist. Assuming all teams have an equal chance of winning the pennant in their league, the odds of the Cubs and Sox meeting in the Series are roughly 1.5 percent. (So, you're telling me there's a chance!) Could the universe be cruel enough to let this series happen in the year that Cubs and Sox fans could not actually ride the Red Line up and down and attend the games? Still, even without fans in the parks, or the Series being played in Chicago, it would be enormous fun, were it not for the distinct chance the Sox would come out on top. (As of yesterday, FanGraphs gave the Sox (5.7 percent) a slightly better chance than the Cubs (5.5 percent) to win the World Series.)

Both teams currently have only two first-rate starters—Yu Darvish and Kyle Hendricks for the Cubs; Dallas Keuchel and Lucas Giolito for the Sox. After that, both teams' third starters have serious questions. For the Cubs, it is Jon Lester, who after getting out to a very good start has been giving up runs at an alarming rate lately and will need a substantial reversion to old form to be effective in the postseason. For the Sox, it is Dylan Cease, the former Cub prospect, who has a very nice 3.33 ERA, but appears to be doing it with smoke and mirrors. His FIP (fielding independent pitching), which is the sabermetric analogue to ERA that takes out of the equation the relatively random outcomes of balls put in play, is a much higher 5.92, even worse than Lester's fairly awful 5.61. That kind of discrepancy is a telltale sign of a pitcher who has been more lucky than good. How well he will hold up in postseason play is as much a question for him as it is for Lester. Beyond this point, both teams are trying to patch together rotations crippled by injuries or opt-outs, sidelining starters they had counted on when the season began (e.g., Jose Quintana, Tyler Chatwood, Carlos Rodon, Michael Kopech).

At the plate, the Sox quite clearly have the edge. Jose Abreu is pounding the ball and is leading the league in RBI; Tim Anderson is threatening to lead the league in batting average for the second straight season; and they are getting substantial production from Eloy Jimenez, Luis Robert, James McCann, and Yasmani Grandal. On the Cubs' side, were it not for surprisingly good sprints from Ian Happ and Jason Heyward, and production from David Bote and Jason Kipnis at the bottom of the order, they would be woeful. Anthony Rizzo is having his typically slow first 40 games, and that hurts a lot more in a 60-game season. Javy Baez is swinging and missing more than he ever has (striking out in more than 35 percent of his at bats), and the numbers so far for Kris Bryant, who has hit two home runs, are worse than those of any bad month in his career. Kyle Schwarber is doing about what it appears the Cubs can reasonably expect from him—bat around .230, strike out and walk a lot, and hit home runs at a 35-per-full season rate. The Cubs are worse than the Sox in every hitting category except walks.

And even with significantly more walks than the Sox, the Cubs still have a worse on-base percentage.

If they were to meet in the World Series, it would be great theater. In the first season series between the teams, the Sox took two of three and hit 12 home runs off Cubs pitching (six by Jose Abreu). They managed in just three games to tie two major-league records—home runs in most consecutive at bats in an inning (four) and home runs in consecutive at bats by one player (Abreu, four). The Cubs and Sox finish their seasons with another three-game series, this time on the south side. Both teams could be battling for whatever advantage winning the division affords, but they could also be in the mode of saving their limited starting pitching ammunition for their first-round postseason series. Either way, it will be a fun (and unique) way to end the season in Chicago.

———

MEANWHILE, BASEBALL IN general continues to be entertaining. Wednesday night, Milwaukee beat Detroit 19–0, and it wasn't the day's biggest margin of victory. That distinction went to Atlanta, which beat Miami 29–9. It marked another baseball first this season—the first time any game had ever ended in that score. Among other noteworthy details of that game, the Braves' Adam Duvall hit two-run, three-run, and grand slam homers, in that order, for the first time ever. The last first-ever final score before this one (known by some as a "Scorigami") was in 1999, when the Reds beat the Rockies 24–12.

I don't recall noting the Reds-Rockies game at the time, but I do remember another first-time score (and one that is still unique in baseball history) when the Cubs lost to the Phillies 23–22 on May 17, 1979. It was a day I had promised myself I was finally going to start studying for the upcoming bar exam. But around 1:20 p.m., I turned on the Cubs game, just to watch the first inning—just one inning. The Phillies scored seven in the top of the first. Okay, time to get to studying. But then the Cubs came back with six in their half, and the hook was set. Four hours later, exhausted, I promised myself I would really start studying tomorrow. It was a great game to watch with many memorable twists and details, including a home run deep into the left field bleachers in the 10th inning by Mike Schmidt off Bruce Sutter. Schmidt had two homers in the game (to go with an uncharacteristic two errors), and Dave Kingman hit three for the Cubs. Larry Bowa, who would be the Cubs shortstop in a few years, collected five hits for the Phillies. Maybe the most remarkable statistic, though, is that the Phillies, despite scoring 23 runs, still managed to leave 15 runners on base. Cubs pitching worked out of a lot of jams to keep it close.

The Braves on Wednesday night, in addition to posting a first-ever final score, had a chance to break the modern (i.e., post 1900) MLB record of 30 runs held by the Texas Rangers (who beat Baltimore 30–3 in 2007), but they couldn't score in the eighth, and then as the home team, didn't get the chance to hit in the ninth. The 2007 Rangers game is noteworthy in light of the recent flap they raised when Fernando Tatis Jr. hit a grand slam on a 3–0 count in the eighth inning of a game in which the Padres led the

Rangers 10–3—thus, in the minds of some, violating one of baseball's unwritten rules. In their 30–3 win over the Orioles, the Rangers scored 16 runs in the final two innings, more than doubling the 14–3 lead they held after seven. Apparently, then the unwritten rule gave them no pause in keeping their foot on the pedal in the final two innings of a blowout game.

It was the second time in 10 days that a team needed only one more inning of run production to make history. On the night of September 1, the Giants had scored 23 runs in the first eight innings against the Rockies in Coors Field and had put up at least one run in each of those innings. They were thus on the verge of becoming only the 21st team in MLB history to score in every inning (in which they had a chance to bat) of a nine-inning game, an event rarer than a perfect game. The last team to do so was the White Sox, who scored in the first eight innings against the Indians in 2016, but they were the home team and so didn't bat in the ninth.

The complete nine-inning feat is much rarer. (The chances of a team scoring in every inning of a nine-inning game, as calculated by the Society for American Baseball Research, are one in 225,917.) Since 1900, only three teams have done it, all in the National League. The last time was by the Colorado Rockies against the Chicago Cubs in Wrigley Field on May 5, 1999, thanks to an error by Cubs first baseman Mark Grace in the ninth inning. The Giants scoring in the ninth therefore would have been a true rarity. And it looked very promising. Drew Butera, a catcher/first baseman whose last pitching stint had been one third of an inning in 2018, was on the mound for the Rockies. He gave up a leadoff double to Alex Dickerson on a deep shot to center but then, amazingly, retired the next three hitters on a strikeout, ground out unassisted to first, and a comebacker to Butera. No history for you, San Francisco.

One significant baseball first, albeit one that will have an asterisk attached, could occur in the American League home-run race this year. Since 1900 (and maybe ever), no player has led the league in home runs at age 40 or older, not even the ever-young Barry Bonds (who last did it at age 36 and, remarkably, only twice in his career). Before yesterday, 40-year-old Nelson Cruz was tied with Mike Trout for the American League lead with 15 (a 53-home-run pace over a full season). Trout hit number 16 yesterday to pull ahead by one. Obviously, the betting money in this contest is on Trout (or the field), but I would not sell Cruz short. Last year, at age 39, he hit 41 homers playing in only 120 games. And Cruz is by no means a one-trick pony this year—he is batting .342 and leads the league in slugging (.685) and OPS (1.117). If he can pull it off, it will be an amazing first, even in a 60-game season.

Finally, it is impossible not to mention the remarkable postgame interview given by the ever-irascible Trevor Bauer following the Reds' 3–0 win over the Cubs Wednesday night, in which Bauer threw 7 2/3 innings of three-hit ball, striking out 10 and walking none, before leaving after yielding a couple hits in the bottom of the eighth. As he left the mound, Bauer waved to the Cubs dugout, and the Cubs TV announcers noted that there had been a fair amount of "chirping" directed Bauer's way throughout the game. Bauer was asked about that in the clubhouse after the game.

Baseball fans are inured to the standard cliche-filled post-game interview most players give. Paul Dickson's book *The Unwritten Rules of Baseball* includes a wonderful section collecting, alphabetically, baseball aphorisms, adages, and similar expressions that "define the national pastime." One is "Carmen's List of Responses to Reporters," a list of 37 cliches that Phillies reliever Don Carmen used to keep taped inside his locker door. After the game, he would direct reporters to the list with the comment: "You saw the game, take what you need."

Trevor Bauer is not like Don Carmen, or for that matter most other major-league players. He has strong opinions on most things and is not afraid to express them. He did not disappoint when asked about the dugout wave: "They were yelling at me all night," Bauer said. "It's kind of funny, you know, I've got to give them props. They actually chirped all night and yelled at me all night. Normally when they get behind, they shut up real quick. So I really got to give them props. I mean, even when I got taken out, they're yelling 'bye' at me. So I give them a nice little wave and some other stuff because it was impressive that you can chirp at some-one after he shoved it up your ass for 7 2/3 innings." As Jayson Stark loves to say: Baseball!

Lester

Is Jon Lester headed for the Hall of Fame? Some baseball observers think so, but I am not among them. That is not because his body of work through 2019 is insubstantial. I have a great deal of respect for Lester as a pitcher, a professional, and a team leader. He has had an excellent career; to me, though, he is just not quite Hall-worthy. He currently has 192 career wins over 15 seasons with a very good, though not exceptional, career ERA of 3.59. He is a five-time All-Star but has never won a Cy Young Award (coming closest in 2016 when he was 19–5 with a 2.44 ERA and finished second). His career WAR of 44.6 is very good but well short of the average 73.3 WAR of starting pitchers in the Hall (and also well behind peers Justin Verlander, Clayton Kershaw, Max Scherzer, and Zack Greinke).

Probably the most compelling part of Lester's case is an outstanding ERA of 2.51 in 26 postseason games, and an even better 1.77 in six World Series games on three Series-winning teams. His postseason ERA and WHIP are better than Verlander's, Kershaw's, Scherzer's, and Greinke's. And his performance in the fall has also been better than that of several first-ballot Hall of Fame inductees with substantial postseason experience, including Greg Maddux, Pedro Martinez, and Tom Glavine. Is that enough?

Jay Jaffe, author of *The Cooperstown Casebook* and probably the leading expert among today's baseball scribes on qualifications for the Hall of Fame, rates Lester as coming up short under each of the several metrics he uses to assess players' careers. The one indicator Jaffe looks at that has Lester closest is Bill James's "Hall of Fame Monitor," which uses a multi-factor point system to calculate "how likely (not how deserving) an active player is to make the Hall of Fame." Using this measure, James has Lester at 96 on a scale where 100 is "likely" to get voted in.

Before this year, and before it became clear we would not have a full season, I thought that if Lester was to have a good shot at Cooperstown, he needed at least one more strong season. Unfortunately, this year did not provide that opportunity; the best he could hope to do would be an impressive 60-game partial season, and possibly a further expansion of his extensive postseason resume.

So what about this season? Lester got off to a great start, with three consecutive strong performances, then began surrendering runs at an alarming rate and saw his ERA balloon to above 5.50 before his last start brought it down somewhat. What accounts for this? Opposing hitters' batting average on balls in play against Lester this year is .285, well below his career average of .303 and barely above that of teammate Yu Darvish, who currently has an ERA of 1.77. The explanation for Lester's ineffectiveness must lie in the "three true outcomes"—walks, strikeouts, and home runs.

Through his first eight starts, Lester was averaging 2.2 walks per nine innings, significantly better than his career average of 2.9 and better than any of his last four seasons with the Cubs. So, control has not been the issue. His strike-out rate of 6.5 per nine through those eight starts, however, was the lowest of his career, making this a possible explanation for the substantial run production against him. Although Lester has never been a dominant strikeout pitcher like Scherzer or Verlander, he has averaged around 8.4 per nine over his career. Fewer strikeouts mean more balls in play, and thus more baserunners. But Dallas Keuchel of the White Sox (who walks hitters at about the same rate as Lester) is striking out the fewest batters per nine innings among all MLB pitchers this season, yet has an ERA of 2.19, so that cannot be the only explanation for Lester's poor performance.

That leaves one category: home runs. After giving up one (a solo shot) in his first three starts, Lester served up eight home-run balls in his next five starts, which put him among the four worst starters in baseball in home runs per nine innings. (Dallas Keuchel, by contrast, leads the AL in fewest home runs per nine.) Roughly two-thirds of the runs scored against Lester this year have come via home run. Why has he been so prone to the long ball? One possible explanation is that he is simply not quite as fast as he used to be. His fastball was never overpowering, so the loss of a mile or two off the top end may be enough to let hitters catch it more often. Another, as Lester himself has offered, is that his breaking ball has not been effective in most of his starts. Or it may be that, while he is not walking a lot of hitters, Lester's control *within the strike zone* has been poor—that he is simply throwing too many pitches over the part of the plate where hitters can drive them with authority. Maybe, at age 36, he has simply hit the wall.

The good news for the Cubs, at least temporarily, is that in his last start, on Friday night against the Brewers, Lester ended the home run binge, throwing six innings, striking out eight, and giving up no runs. If the Cubs are to have any chance of making a run deep in the postseason, they will need Lester to pitch at this level. Even if it isn't enough to get him into the Hall of Fame, it could be what the Cubs need to bring a happy ending to their fans before the core of the 2016 championship team starts its inevitable diaspora.

Four Wins

LAST SATURDAY NIGHT, the Chicago Cubs, while still holding first place in their division, did not have the look of a team likely to make any kind of run in the fast-approaching postseason. They had lost six of their last 10 games. And they had been shut out in two of their last three. In the first of these on September 9, Trevor Bauer shut them down for 7 2/3, then mocked the Cubs' "chirping" in his post-game interview. The Cubs managed only three hits in a 3–0 loss. And on Friday night, September 11, they lost to Milwaukee 1–0, a game in which they had only two hits and struck out 16 times. Although their starting pitching remained solid, after that game the batting averages of the four biggest sluggers in the heart of the Cubs lineup were still hovering around the Mendoza line.

But despite the sinking feeling that had begun to settle in among their fans, the Cubs have just won four in a row to right the ship. And they have done so in four completely different, all highly entertaining, ways.

Win #1—Saturday night, the 12th, looked like it was going to be one more case of the Cubs going down with barely a whimper against the Milwaukee Brewers. Through eight innings, the Cubs had four hits and no runs. Josh Hader came in to pitch the ninth inning to hold the Brewers' 2–0 lead. Hader is one of the most dominating left-handed relievers in the game. In 14 games this season, he had given up just two hits and no home runs. After Kyle Schwarber bunted foul on strike three to lead off the inning, the Cubs' statistical chances of winning the game were 4 percent, but against Hader, with two left-handed hitters coming up after Javy Baez, they were actually lower than that.

And then, one of those things happened that makes us remember why we don't just turn off the game and go to bed. Baez lined a single to the opposite field, and Anthony Rizzo followed with a choked-up single ripped to right after falling behind 0–2. This brought Jason Heyward to the plate—Heyward, who had repeatedly disappointed Cubs fans as a hitter since joining the team in 2016 but is having probably his best season as a Cub. As he had with Rizzo, Hader got ahead with two strikes, but on his fourth pitch Heyward drove the ball deep to right-center field for a three-run homer. Then, to cap off a highly improbable 15 minutes, Ildemaro Vargas, a journeyman utility player the Cubs had just picked up on waivers, connected for another home run off Hader, giving the Cubs a 4–2 lead.

In a situation that raised the distinct possibility of disaster, David Ross brought in Craig Kimbrel to pitch the bottom of the ninth. Kimbrel, not without a few nervous moments, was up to the task. After yielding hits to the first two Milwaukee batters, he retired the next three to earn only his second save of the season and secure an unlikely win.

Win #2—The following afternoon, the Cubs hitters awoke and parlayed 10 hits and seven walks into a 12-run outburst. But the story of the game was the Cubs' starting pitcher, Alec Mills, a 22nd round draft pick by the Kansas City Royals in 2012 making just his 15th major-league start (12th for the Cubs over three seasons). Before this day, he had never thrown a complete game. But on Sunday, September 13, he threw the 16th no hitter in Cubs history. It was the second no hitter of the Covid-19 season, the other being thrown by Lucas Giolito of the Chicago White Sox. This strange, short season thus became the first one (in the 120 years of the teams' common existence) in which both a Cubs and Sox pitcher accomplished this feat in the same season.

Not all no hitters are thrown by great pitchers, and not all great pitchers throw no hitters; but all no hitters are special to the man on the mound when that 27th out gets recorded. This one came on a ground ball up the middle to a perfectly positioned Javy Baez, who flashed a smile (reminiscent of Kris Bryant's on the final out of the 2016 World Series) before he had even released his throw to first for the final out. Pandemic-imposed social distancing protocol was temporarily suspended as Mills's teammates mobbed him on the field.

Win #3—The Cubs played the first of a two-game set with their 2016 World Series opponents, the Cleveland Indians, on Tuesday, September 15th. It was a taut, seesaw game in which the five plays with the greatest impact on the potential outcome of the game all occurred in the eighth and ninth innings. As Cubs announcer Jim Deshaies noted, the game would have been an "instant classic" had it been played in the postseason.

What stood out most from at least this Cubs fan's perspective was that the key plays of the game (until the final bizarre climax), involved the Cubs players who were at the core of that 2016 championship team and who have been underperforming for most of this season. Bryant, Rizzo, Contreras, and Baez collected eight of the Cubs' 11 hits; Bryant and Baez scored five of their six runs; and Bryant, Rizzo, Contreras, and Baez all had RBI. And the emblematic play of the game was Javy Baez adding to his career highlight reel in the bottom of the eighth when he attempted to steal second and, after the throw got loose and the ball skittered into short left center, popped to his feet and motored all the way around to score when the throw home eluded catcher Sandy Leon.

The game could not be a Cubs-Indians "classic" without the Cubs bullpen blowing a lead late in the game, which was exactly what happened. Jeremy Jeffress, who has been a reliable closer for the Cubs, came in to protect a 5–3 lead in the bottom of the ninth. With one out and one on, Cleveland's superstar shortstop Francisco Lindor drove a line drive into the empty bleachers in left to tie the game.

In the bottom of the ninth, after Bryant walked with one out and Rizzo singled up the middle, Cleveland brought in Nick Wittgren to pitch to Willson Contreras. Wittgren, a hard thrower, ordinarily has pretty good control, but not this night. His first pitch was hard, high, and tight, inducing a (perhaps exaggerated) drop to the dirt by Contreras after it sailed under his chin, followed by an icy glare toward the mound. Contreras took a full cut at the next pitch, again a high fastball, and missed. The third pitch was another wayward two-seamer that nailed Contreras on the body armor. After flinging the bat toward the dugout in disgust, Contreras made his way unhappily toward first, where Rizzo had waited just to make sure there was no trouble. Calmness prevailed, Rizzo proceeded to second base, and Cameron Maybin, the Cubs' recent trade-deadline acquisition, stepped to the plate with the bases loaded, looking to become a fresh Cub hero. But he didn't get the chance. As if to prove that he had not intentionally thrown at Contreras, Wittgren drilled Maybin in the ribs with his first pitch, forcing in Bryant and giving the Cubs a rare walk-off-hit-by-pitch victory.

Win #4—The Cubs and Indians played another good, tight game the next night. This one featured the best and the worst of this year's Cubs. Jon Lester started for the Cubs, coming off an excellent performance in his last outing. While he yielded only two runs, Lester was dodging bullets almost from the first batter, as hitter after hitter in the Indians lineup hit the ball *hard*. Only good fortune turned many of those shots into outs. Lester's designated catcher from the 2016 season, now the Cubs' clear-eyed manager, removed him after five innings, even though he had thrown only 62 pitches, with the game tied 2–2.

The Cubs had briefly taken a 2–1 lead in the bottom of the fourth on another burst of Javy Baez magic. With one out and a man on first, Baez hit a ground ball to short that looked like it would produce a double play. But with Javy running hard to first, the relay throw was in the dirt and hit him on the heel as he reached the bag. When the ball bounced into short right, Baez took off for second, and without ever slowing down continued to third, beating the throw easily. He went on to score on an infield hit, a run that resulted, for the second time in two days, from Javy's aggressive base running.

While the game remained tied at 2–2 through nine, it is worth noting that Craig Kimbrel pitched a 1-2-3 eighth, striking out two of the three Cleveland hitters he faced. Although he has had a few rough outings, largely attributable to poor control, there is nothing wrong with Kimbrel's arm. His fastball is consistently hitting 97 and his curve, when he controls it, is virtually unhittable. In 14 innings pitched this season, he has struck out 26 batters. After his last two performances, it will be interesting to see if he can perform well enough during the Cubs' remaining regular season games for Ross to be willing to trust him in high-leverage situations once the postseason begins.

The game moved into extra innings. Despite the new rule spotting the Indians a runner at second to start the inning, relatively untested reliever Jason Adam was able to escape the top of the tenth without yielding a run. The Cubs started their half with Ian Happ on second, who then advanced to third on a Kris Bryant single. Cleveland, with right-hander Phil Maton pitching, sensibly issued an intentional walk to Anthony Rizzo to load the bases with no outs. Due up: Contreras, Schwarber, and Baez.

The next 10 minutes was the Cubs season in microcosm. Needing to put the ball in play, preferably in the air, Contreras struck out on three pitches. Schwarber, after working the count to 2–2, also flailed and missed for strike three. That brought up Baez. On the first two pitches he swung as hard as possible at high fastballs, missing both.

Cubs fans all know how the movie goes from here: breaking ball low and away, inducing a dispiriting, inning-ending swing and miss. Maton knew the script and threw a curve at least eight inches off the outside corner, but he didn't get it down. Javy lunged out across the plate, flicked the bat, and somehow managed to pull-hook that outside pitch over the third baseman's head into left field for the Cubs' second consecutive walk-off win. Whew.

So, this is the state of the Cubs team with nine games left to play before the postseason begins. I cannot hazard a guess at how far they will go—there are simply too many variables and too many uncertainties about which Cubs team will show up. But at least the last four wins have given a glimmer of hope to the notion that the magic just might come together for a couple weeks at the right time so that the Cubs could be spending late October in Texas.

The Bryson DeChambeau of Baseball

G OLFER BRYSON DECHAMBEAU won the U.S. Open golf tournament last week playing the classic Winged Foot course in a way that was highly idiosyncratic and to many, before it worked, suicidal—by hitting the ball as far as he could, regardless of whether it ended up in the short grass of the fairway or the deep, thick rough. While his approach off the tee had all the finesse of a cudgel, his unique and thoroughly analyzed approach allowed him to beat the best golfers in the world on an extremely difficult golf course. In doing so, he surpassed, by a wide margin, the record for fewest number of fairways hit by a U.S. Open champion.

Following the U.S. Open, Joe Posnanski published an excellent story on DeChambeau in *The Athletic*. Comparing him to James Harden in the NBA, Posnanski describes how DeChambeau decided to become the best in his sport by taking a completely different approach and not giving a damn what anybody thought of it, or for that matter whether they liked him much. Thus, he went on an aggressive weight-gaining regimen combined with a rigorous workout routine that bulked him up by 40 pounds to a player who looks more like he should be playing middle linebacker in the NFL than playing golf on the PGA tour. He was already known for his cerebral approach to the game—nobody thinks about and analyzes the golf swing more than DeChambeau. For example, he had previously gained attention for deciding that it made sense to play with a set of irons all the same length, unlike every other player on tour. This season, his analysis led him to adopt a very basic approach: perfect a power swing that can hit the ball farther off the tee than anybody else and then go out and hit it as far as he can on almost every hole.

Trevor Bauer has followed a similarly individualistic path in major-league baseball. After he played college ball at UCLA, the Arizona Diamondbacks drafted Bauer with the third overall pick in 2011. He came up in 2012 at age 21 and started four late-season games without distinguishing himself. Arizona then promptly traded their top pick to the Cleveland Indians after that season. He saw only limited action the next season with Cleveland, again starting just four games.

But since 2014, his age-23 season, he has been a full-time member of the starting rotation—first for Cleveland and now for Cincinnati. In the first four of those seasons, he did not post an ERA below 4.18, though he had a winning record of 45–37. Even in the best of those years, 2017, when he went 17–9 Bauer did not register in the Cy Young voting at the end of the year. He struck out a fair number of hitters, but he had just an average WHIP that never went below 1.300. In short, he was a good, middle-of-the-rotation starter, but one who was not overpowering and appeared to have limited upside.

Then in 2018, Bauer had a breakout season with Cleveland. He had an ERA of 2.21, second best in the league in mid-August, when a line drive off the bat of Jose Abreu broke his right leg and cost him the rest of the season. That year, he dropped his WHIP to an excellent 1.089, led the league in fielding independent pitching (which measures those aspects of pitching over which the pitcher has the most control), averaged more than 11 strikeouts per nine, and gave up a league-low 0.5 home runs per nine. He finished sixth in Cy Young voting. He regressed in 2019, doing especially poorly after being traded in late-July from Cleveland to Cincinnati. But he bounced back in the shortened 2020 season to put up spectacular numbers: In 11 starts, he had a 1.71 ERA, threw two shutouts, led the league in WHIP (0.79), and finished just four behind Jacob deGrom for most strikeouts. He is among the leading contenders to win this year's Cy Young award.

Bauer describes himself as being one of the least physically gifted pitchers in the major leagues. When he started pitching in high school, where the prospects who catch scouts' attention can now throw over 90 mph, Bauer could not even hit 80. So how did a player with a lack of physical gifts go on to be the third pick in the draft, then post several years of mediocrity in the big leagues, and this year become one of the favorites to win the Cy Young Award in the National League? As Bauer explains it: "I was made."

The making of Trevor Bauer is chronicled in *The MVP Machine: How Baseball's New Nonconformists Are Using Data to Build Better Players*, by Ben Lindberg and Travis

Sawchick. Bauer, like DeChambeau, is an intellectual tinkerer, who early in life rejected the notion of blindly accepting the advice of experts on how to learn pitching. As they describe Bauer's view on advice: "It's not that he won't listen, Bauer says, it's that he rejects bad advice. He explains that he's very coachable if someone is presenting useful information and can explain its logic. . . . He wants to know the logic or science behind any practice or drill." Asked what it is that made his son a successful major league pitcher, Bauer's father Warren explained that he has "grit," a personality trait associated by some psychologists with a "growth mindset" that allows some people to achieve beyond their apparent limits. Trevor Bauer epitomizes growth mindset; he decided as a teenager to figure out how to be better than his natural talent and early performance showed he could reasonably expect to be.

The coupling of Bauer's rejection of conventional baseball wisdom with a burning growth mindset led him to seek out teachers, mostly sports iconoclasts, whose methods could be explained so that they made sense to him. Lindberg and Sawchick describe how, when he was 10, Bauer began working with a pitching coach named Alan Jaeger, who was an advocate of long-toss training—building arm strength by repeatedly making very long throws. Several years later, his father took him to the Texas Baseball Ranch, a hole-in-the-wall operation run by Ron Wolforth, who employed a series of unusual techniques including use of weighted balls and high frame-rate video to analyze throwing mechanics. By the time he was a junior in high school, Bauer's pitch speed had gone from 76 to 94.

It was at the Texas Baseball Ranch that Bauer came to understand and apply the concept of "tunneling." When a 90-mph pitch leaves the pitcher's hand, the batter has roughly 125 milliseconds to decide whether to swing. That is when the ball is barely a third of the way to the plate. If a pitcher can throw every pitch so that it travels the same path for that first 20 feet, it is extremely difficult for the batter to identify the type of pitch that is coming. Bauer trained with a device that held a metal frame with a 13" x 10" opening placed 20 feet from the mound. He worked on trying to throw all his pitches from the same release point through this imaginary window so that each one would look the same to the hitter at that microsecond when he has to decide whether to swing and at what.

Through working at the Texas Baseball Ranch, Bauer met Kyle Boddy, who runs Driveline Baseball (outside Seattle, Washington). When the two first met, Boddy was already deeply into both the analytics of the baseball pitching motion and developing training regimens to maximize the potential of pitchers' arms. Like Wolforth, Boddy believed strongly in having pitchers develop arm strength by throwing heavy balls, which he was convinced would allow pitchers' arms to both achieve and endure greater peak force when throwing a baseball. Ultimately, Boddy believed that fundamental changes in training and arm motion could do two things that would make a pitcher more effective: increase velocity and increase spin rate. Bauer understood what Boddy was saying, and it made sense to him. As a result, that is where Bauer spends every offseason, working on turning a mediocre raw product into the best pitcher in baseball.

At Driveline Baseball, Boddy and his staff pioneered the use of a high-speed camera, the Edgertronic SC1, to measure release point, spin rate, pitch trajectory, and so on. Here is how Bauer uses the Edgertronic camera, as described by Lindberg and Sawchick: "Examining the view between sets of pitches, Bauer sees the ball first lose contact with his thumb and then separate from his middle finger. His spiked index finger, its fingertip and nail raised vertical and jabbed into the surface, touch the ball last before it flies, subtly altering the axis of its spin. If he times this sequence just right, he'll create the perfect spin axis and produce the pitch movement he wants." That is how Bauer works on each pitch in his arsenal.

Like DeChambeau, Bauer is pretty much a loner among his professional peers, in part because he is so focused on his craft. He says it's not that he's unwilling to talk to or help out his teammates; they just don't seek out his input all that much. And like DeChambeau, he really doesn't care what anybody else thinks about how he goes about his baseball business. A *Sports Illustrated* feature story on him in 2019 aptly bore the title "Trevor Bauer Is More Concerned About Being Right Than Being Liked." In 2018, he was open about saying that he should have won the Cy Young award, despite the injury that ended his season early. He was just as open in saying he'd had a better season than his teammate Corey Kluber, who finished ahead of him in the voting. And in mid-September 2020, with the prospect that his Reds team might soon be facing the Cubs in the post-season, Bauer was happy in postgame interviews to needle the Cubs for "chirping" at him during the game he had just pitched against them, saying it was "impressive" that the

Cubs could chirp at a guy "after he shoved it up your ass for 7 2/3 innings."

So, no—Trevor Bauer is not overly concerned about being liked. But he is determined to pitch his own way and to become the best pitcher in baseball by doing so. And along the way he is going to say exactly what he thinks. Whether Bryson DeChambeau's unique approach to the game of golf will make him the number one player in the world remains to be seen. So, too, with Trevor Bauer—we will see if anybody ever says he is the best pitcher in the game. But with both, it will be interesting watching them try.

World Series Preview?

THE CUBS JUST completed their season-ending, three-game series with the White Sox, which at least some Chicago fans hope will be the prelude to a World Series matchup. Going into the series the Cubs were almost certain to win the NL Central, but the White Sox were in a heated competition with Minnesota and Cleveland for the top spot in the AL Central. So, in addition to its appeal as a potential World Series preview, the three-game set also mattered to the regular season. Even if it hadn't, there is enough history between these two teams that the games came with inherent drama regardless of the immediate stakes.

The first game featured Cy Young-candidate Yu Darvish against Dylan Cease, the hard-throwing young pitcher the Cubs had traded (along with top hitting prospect Eloy Jimenez) to the Sox for veteran starter Jose Quintana. The uneven performance of Quintana and the emergence of Jimenez as a legitimate power hitter suggests that that deal would be a good one for the Sox, straight up. The jury is still out on whether Cease will couple control with his outstanding stuff and make this trade go down as an absolute *steal* for the Sox.

Two of the stories in Chicago during the short season have been the Sox' prolific offensive production, on the one hand—and the Cubs' lack of offense, on the other. Going into the year-end series, the Sox as a team were hitting .261, and they led the AL with 90 home runs and a .453 slugging percentage. The Cubs, by contrast, were batting .220, slugging an anemic .387, and had hit only 65 home runs. So, of course, the Cubs won the first game 10–0, hitting five home runs, while Darvish and two relievers held the potent White Sox offense to three harmless hits.

Of those five Cubs home runs, one stood out: Willson Contreras's three-run shot in the third inning, which he punctuated with a bat flip that must surely hold the altitude record for this or (apologies to Jose Bautista) likely any other season. A propitious camera angle caught the bat's upwards pinwheeling trajectory against the night sky, with the flight of his high drive to right field clearly visible behind it. The camera's perspective made it appear the bat had the superior apogee. As might have been predicted, the Sox did not bear the Contreras bat flip happily. Contreras walked on four pitches his next time up, but when he came to the plate in the seventh inning Sox reliever Jimmy Cordero hit him in the ribs. After a brief conference, the umpires ejected both Cordero and Sox manager Rick Renteria. Contreras got the last laugh by homering again in his final at bat to put the cherry on the drubbing, this time politely dropping the bat near home plate before circling the bases.

The second game was a different story, as the White Sox bats came alive. The Cubs had grabbed a 5–2 lead in the top of the third on a long grand slam by Kris Bryant, only his third home run of the season. But then Jon Lester, likely making his last regular season start for the Cubs, could not get through the fourth inning. He left after giving up two hits and three walks, the last walk forcing in a run, and leaving the bases loaded for reliever Ryan Tepera. The first hitter to face Tepera was Jose Abreu, who may well win the American League MVP and showed why—by doubling to clear the bases and put the Sox up 7–5. The Cubs could do nothing the rest of the way, while the Sox tacked on two more with a Yoan Moncada home run and won the game 9–5.

The final game of the season on Sunday may have been the most entertaining of the three. The Cubs jumped all over Sox starter Reynaldo Lopez for six runs in the second inning, which included home runs from Kris Bryant and David Bote and a steal of home by Billy Hamilton for the final run of the inning. Hamilton, making the most of a rare start, then homered in the fourth to put the Cubs up 7–0, making the game start to look very much like the series opener. Billy Hamilton Day continued in the seventh, with the Cubs holding a 7–1 lead, when he singled, stole second, advanced to third on a wild pitch, and then scored on a dribbler in front of the plate off Kris Bryant's bat. It was 10–1 after seven. But the Sox fought back with five runs in the eighth, scored two with nobody out in the ninth on a Yasmani Grandal homer, and put another man on, bringing Nomar Mazara to the plate as the tying run. To the relief of Cubs fans, reliever Andrew Chafin got Mazara to take strike three and end the game 10–8.

Taking two out of three from the Sox feels like a good lead-in to the postseason. Two of the Cubs starters, Darvish and Adbert Alzolay, had excellent outings (the Sox scoring in Alzolay's start on Sunday came late, after he left), and maybe more importantly, the Cubs hit in all three games. They scored 25 runs and hit nine home runs in the series, giving at least some indication that the Cubs' marquee players may be coming out of their 57-game funk. While other teams clearly look better on paper, it is not hard to believe the Cubs have a chance to make a serious run.

PART TWO

The Postseason

And Now, the Rest of the Season

September 29

ALMOST MIRACULOUSLY, MAJOR-LEAGUE baseball managed to complete its 60-game season despite a couple extended interruptions of several teams' schedules by Covid-19 outbreaks. Most of those were early, before the teams and their players got more serious about adhering to the league's protocols and limiting player interactions with the outside, potentially infected, world. Every team got in all 60 games, except for the Cardinals and Tigers, who played 58. It required seven-inning doubleheader games to get there, but it is still pretty remarkable.

The games were played in empty stadiums, which at first was disconcerting but eventually revealed unexpected advantages. Most prominent of these was that the usually inaudible sounds of the game suddenly became quite audible. Fans thus were treated to hearing players communicating with teammates on the field and sometimes to hearing opposing players mouthing off at each other. And there were numerous ejections this year of players on the benches (or in the stands), whose critiques of umpiring performance were no longer drowned out by crowd noise. The absence of fans also contributed to the completion of the season because it allowed teams to reschedule start times on very short notice to dodge bad weather or accommodate travel problems, and hence avoid postponements that would have added to the already substantial burden of making up the games lost to Covid-19.

The 2020 season will, in the minds of most fans, always be viewed as an inadequate substitute for the 162-game season and all that it entails. And it was, even to those of us who thoroughly enjoyed having even 37 percent of a whole season. Some players put up great performances for 60 games, but there is no guarantee they could have continued performing at those levels for a full season. (One need only think of all the All-Stars in years past whose second halves faded to dim shadows of the numbers they put up before the Fourth of July.) And conversely, there are a number of very good players who had miserable 60-game seasons, but who might well have surged to put up big numbers if they had had another 100 games to play. Last year, Yu Darvish was one of the worst pitchers in the National League in the first half of the season; he may have been the best in the second half. So, too, with the teams. The Washington Nationals had the same record after their first 50 games this year as they did last season (19-31). This year, they didn't make the 16-game postseason; last year they went on to win the World Series.

But to those who can get past the obvious artificiality of the truncated "season," there were a lot of good stories to watch play out. Back in mid-August, I lamented that we would not get to see a full season of play by some of baseball's rising stars—young players who had already made a mark on the game. Still, a few of them gave us a tantalizing taste of what is to come. Juan Soto (won NL batting title and led the majors with 1.185 OPS), Ronald Acuna (.250/.406/.581), Fernando Tatis Jr. (17 home runs and 45 RBI), and Eloy Jimenez (.296, 14 home runs and 41 RBI) each had outstanding 60-game stretches. Mike Trout (17 HR and 46RBI) had, for him, a subpar two months with an OPS of "only" .993—numbers any other major leaguer would be happy to claim. Nelson Cruz, at age 40, hung tough in the AL home-run race before fading in the last couple of weeks, but still finished the season with an OPS of .992—more than 100 points above his career average. And Bryce Harper, the subject of Mike Petriello's piece analyzing his spectacular start, finished the year with a slash line of .268/.420/.542, for an impressive .962 OPS (well above his career average), more walks than strikeouts for the first time in his career, and an xBA of .307.

For other players, the short season was highly disappointing. Christian Yelich, who had led the league in batting average, slugging percentage, and OPS in both of the last two seasons, posted an anemic slash line of .205/.356/.430. And JD Martinez, whose OPS averaged over 1.000 the last three seasons, saw that metric fall more than 300 points to a very sorry .680 this year. A couple of players working on burnishing their Cooperstown cases—Joey Votto and Jon Lester—failed to do so. Votto hit .226 with the lowest OBP of his career, while Lester (5.16 ERA) finished with his career-worst strikeouts and home runs per nine innings. Finally, Shohei Ohtani's season, which looked so promising on July 23, can only be termed a complete bust. In 44 games, he batted .190 and slugged .366. As a pitcher, he appeared in only two games before being shut down. In those games, he pitched 1 2/3 innings, walked eight, and gave up seven earned runs. Nobody mistook him for Babe Ruth this year.

For a season that lasted only two months, it was filled with of all kinds of great, crazy stuff. The new rules, like them or not, produced a series of notable baseball firsts. But even without these gimmicks, there were plenty of "regular" baseball events to cheer. Two pitchers, both playing for Chicago teams, threw the only two no-hitters of the season—the first time pitchers from the Cubs and Sox had done that in the same season. A young star hitter's grand slam, on a 3–0 pitch late in a game when his team had a big lead, prompted several days of vigorous debate over the continued viability of baseball's "unwritten rules," as did the White Sox' intentional plunking of Willson Contreras after he punctuated a home run with a moon-shot bat flip.

Consistent with the trend of recent seasons, we saw prodigious home-run production by individuals (including Jose Abreu coming to the plate with a chance to be the first major leaguer to hit home runs in five consecutive at bats) and teams (including the Yankees hitting five in an inning and the White Sox having a chance to be the first team ever to hit five in a row in an inning). Atlanta became the first team ever to win by a score of 29–9, just missing the modern record for most runs in a game (30). And San Francisco went into the ninth inning with the chance to become only the fourth team since 1900 to score in all nine innings, but were unable, after scoring 23 in the first eight innings, to push one across against Colorado's backup catcher.

Now, baseball is embarking on a wholly unfamiliar postseason. All sixteen teams are playing best-of-three elimination series—no byes, and with just whatever advantage accompanies playing in one's own empty home park going to those with the best records. It feels a little like sweet sixteen weekend in the NCAA basketball tournament. On Wednesday there will be *eight* playoff games being televised (with the possibility of just as many games the next day). If you have nothing else to do (or even if you do), you could go on a postseason bender over those two days.

Is This the End for the Cubs? (Spoiler: Yes)

F OR THE CHICAGO Cubs, rain postponed their day of reckoning with the Miami Marlins after losing the first Wild Card game to the Marlins Wednesday night 5–1. The Cubs led that game 1–0 on Ian Happ's solo home run in the fifth inning, but Kyle Hendricks gave up a three-run homer to Corey Dickerson in the seventh inning, which the Marlins followed with a Jesus Aguilar two-run shot off Hendricks's replacement, Jeremy Jeffress. Meanwhile, the Cubs bats returned to somnolence, managing only one hit after the Happ home run in the fifth.

No one in Chicago needs to be reminded of 2003, the last time the Cubs played the Marlins in the postseason. That series ended with two of the most painful games in Cubs history, when the Cubs needed one win to go to the World Series: first, the meltdown in the eighth inning of Game 6, the infamous Bartman game; followed by a Game 7 in which Kerry Wood, still in his prime, was on the mound, hit a game-tying home run to drive the crowd into ecstasy— and the Cubs still lost. Going into this season, the Marlins have the distinction of being the only team that has won the World Series each year they have made the postseason. The Cubs do not want to facilitate even the slim possibility of Miami making a remarkable piece of baseball history by going three for three.

Of course, all Cubs fans want to win this game and avoid another abrupt end to their World Series chances, but in addition to avoiding elimination, there is the added ingredient of tomorrow's starting pitcher for the Cubs in the deciding game: Jon Lester. Almost everyone (except those with a combination of pessimism and compassion) wants to see Lester get one more start in Wrigley Field, as his career as a Cub likely is at an end when this season is over. Lester has a 2.51 ERA in 26 career postseason games, and in his 12 games for the Cubs he has given up only 19 earned runs. Cubs fans are hoping Lester has at least one big postseason start left in his quickly emptying tank. It will be a compelling story regardless of the outcome.

————

ELSEWHERE, THE "WILD Card Round" has produced some interesting baseball. Cleveland, which was swept in two games by the Yankees, had an excellent 1–2 starting pitching combination with Shane Bieber and Carlos Carrasco. The Yankees, defying the adage that good pitching stops good hitting, knocked both Bieber and Carrasco out early and scored 22 runs in their two wins against the Indians. Cincinnati, which had been hot coming into the postseason and was viewed by many as a team with a chance to make a deep run, lost in two straight to Atlanta without scoring a single run.

It was no surprise that Los Angeles, which had the best 2020 record, swept the sub-.500 Milwaukee Brewers. The big story in that series was Clayton Kershaw, who last night pitched eight masterful innings, giving up only three hits and striking out 13 in a 3–0 win. Kershaw has been the best pitcher in baseball for the last decade but had a losing record and a 4.22 ERA in 32 prior postseason games through 2019. Last night provided one piece of evidence to counter the claim that he cannot pitch in these high-stakes games. Kershaw's less-than-stellar postseason record remains a mystery, a mystery compounded by his excellent 1.076 WHIP over those 32 games.

Houston, another team that made the postseason with a sub-.500 record, pulled off a somewhat surprising sweep of the Minnesota Twins, who had an excellent season. The result was only *somewhat* surprising for two reasons. First, although they hit poorly through most of the 60-game season, the Astros' hitters in the heart of their lineup—Springer, Altuve, Bregman, Correa, and Guriel—are the same ones who anchored a team that won the 2017 World Series and won 107 games in 2019, and they had come to life at the end of the first 60 games. The loss of Verlander to injury (and Cole previously to free agency) make them less likely to prevail in a longer series, but they had the two starters they needed to beat Minnesota. The second reason their win was only somewhat surprising is that Minnesota came into this series having lost their last 16 postseason games. The count is now 18. Houston thus remains the front runner among teams in the postseason that most people would like to see lose.

The White Sox lost the rubber game of their series with Oakland today 6-4. The Sox were one of the best hitting teams in baseball this season, but they went out doing a dead-on imitation of the Cubs—they put lots of runners on base, and failed to get the big hit to bring them in. I was sorry to see them go; I really was holding out the (faint) hope of a Chicago World Series, albeit played in Texas.

The most compelling series of this first round has been the Cardinals and Padres. The Cardinals had by far the toughest path to the postseason, given how many games they lost to Covid-19 quarantine and the resulting flurry of double headers they had to play over the final few weeks of the season. And the Padres are one of the more exciting teams in baseball, with the electric talent of Fernando Tatis Jr. and Manny Machado. Tatis Jr., who hit two home runs last night, looked like a warrior, with his painted face and wide headband holding back his golden dreadlocks. Will Myers also homered twice, making them only the second pair of teammates in MLB history to homer twice in a post-season game (Gehrig and Ruth being the other pair in 1932). The victory marked the Padres' first postseason win in Petco Park, which opened in 2004, having lost four straight play-off games there before this—all to the Cardinals. Their finale tonight should be entertaining.

Finally, these games have provided a reminder of just how slow some postseason games can be as the pace of play seems to grind almost to a halt. The White Sox' Game 3 with Oakland took 4:09 to resolve. And the Padres 11–9 win over the Cardinals, which admittedly did have a fair amount of scoring, extended to 4:19. These postseason games are often filled with strategy, tension, and twists of fortune. But once they run to four hours, the attention spans of even the most dedicated fans start to be tested.

———————

It was indeed the final game for the Cubs, who ended their season losing to the Marlins tonight 2–0. Like Hendricks before him, Darvish held the Marlins scoreless through six innings but yielded two runs in the seventh before departing. This time the Cubs managed five hits, four of them coming from Ian Happ and Jason Heyward, who have been their two most reliable hitters this season. In the two games, Rizzo, Bryant, Baez, Schwarber, and Contreras—who had combined for more than 300 extra-base hits in 2019—went 2-for-32, without a single extra-base hit. The bottom of the ninth inning was a fitting coda to the Cubs season. Heyward led off the inning with a line drive double to left. But the incipient rally quickly died as the next three hitters—Baez, Bote, and Kipnis—all struck out, two of them looking, to bring down the curtain on this season.

Cubs fans could take some small solace from the Cardinals losing to the San Diego Padres 4–0. The game was remarkable in that San Diego used nine pitchers to shut out the Cardinals on just four hits. Austin Adams earned the win by striking out the only batter he faced, in the fifth inning. This nine-pitcher shutout may end up being unique, but given the format for the LDS and LCS, which will have no off days, I suspect that even with the three-batter rule for relievers, there are going to be a lot of games with large casts of pitchers making appearances.

Dynasty? Don't Talk About Dynasty

B Y MOST MEASURES of success in baseball, it is hard to characterize the Chicago Cubs' last six years as anything but successful. They won the 2016 World Series with a team that had the best starting pitching and defense in baseball and a lineup that included Anthony Rizzo, 24-year-old MVP Kris Bryant and a handful of other young hitters, including Javier Baez, Willson Contreras, and Kyle Schwarber, who appeared to be on the cusp of blossoming into stars. Their record over those six years was 505–365, for a winning percentage of .580. In their worst regular season, 2019, they went 84–78. They made the postseason five of those six years and played in the NLCS three consecutive seasons. And yet, after this season, I suspect most Cubs fans feel (as they did after last season) that the Cubs have significantly underachieved. They have not built a dynasty.

Chicago sports fans have seen this kind of thing before. Thirty years before the Cubs' World Series win, the Chicago Bears won the 1986 Super Bowl in a romp over the thoroughly overmatched New England Patriots, after going

15–1 in the 1985 regular season. The Bears team that year featured one of the best defenses of all time, with a fearsome front line of Dan Hampton, Richard Dent, Steve McMichael, and William (Refrigerator) Perry, who were still relatively early in their careers. They were supported by an equally skilled secondary anchored by Hall of Fame middle linebacker Mike Singletary and other outstanding members of the defense, including Gary Fencik, Wilber Marshall, Otis Wilson, and Dave Duerson. On offense they had a brash, talented, and extremely confident young quarterback in Jim McMahon; the best running back in the game, Walter Payton; and dangerous receivers in Willie Gault and Dennis McKinnon. The Bears, with their young talent and several key veterans who appeared to have a number of good years left, looked like a team destined to return to and win several more Super Bowls; they looked like a dynasty waiting to happen.

But that Bears team, even though most of the core players remained for several more years, did not win any more Super Bowls. Indeed, although they reached the playoffs in five of the next six seasons, winning the NFC Central division four of those years, never played in another Super Bowl. (The Bears' other Super Bowl appearance did not come until 2007, when all of the '85 Bears were long gone.) In the 1986 regular season, the Bears were 14–2 but lost their first-round playoff game at home to the Washington Redskins. The next year, after going 11–4, they again lost in the first round, again at home. And after winning their division for a fourth consecutive year going 12–4 in 1988 and winning their first-round playoff game against Philadelphia in the Fog Bowl, the Bears got crushed in Soldier Field 28–3 by San Francisco in the NFC championship game. Although they had an injury-riddled losing season in 1989, they returned to the playoffs for the next two years—losing in the divisional round to the Giants in 1990 and then losing the Wild Card game at home to Dallas the following year. In the six years after winning the Super Bowl, the Bears' postseason record was 2–5.

The Chicago Cubs' performance after their World Series win is eerily similar to that of the Bears. The Cubs won the NL Central the following year, eked out a 3–2 NLDS win over Washington in a wild fifth game, but then got trounced by the Dodgers in the NLCS. The following year, they tied Milwaukee for the division title but lost the one-game tie breaker to the Brewers (at home) and followed that up by losing (again at home) to Colorado in the Wild Card game. In 2019, a late season collapse that included four straight home losses to the Cardinals caused them to miss the post-season entirely (despite having a 75 percent chance of making it just two weeks before the end of the season). And, of course, this year, they got eliminated in the Wild Card round when they lost two straight games at Wrigley Field after again finishing first in their division.

Much has been written about why the Cubs have not fared better in the postseason since the 2016 World Series win, giving due consideration to the vagaries of short series and the inevitable ebbs and flows of hitters' performance over a small number of games. The analysis inevitably returns to the fact that their best hitters have performed poorly when it counted most. And the other thing that stands out is how awful the Cubs have been in Wrigley Field past mid-September. Counting the one-game tie breaker with Milwaukee, the Cubs have played nine postseason games in Wrigley Field since 2016. They have gone 2–7 in those games. And here are the Cubs' run totals for those home games going back to 2017: 2, 0, 1, 3, 1, 1, 1, 1, 0—10 runs in nine games. Add to that the last four home games in late September of the 2019 season, all of which they lost to St. Louis to bury their postseason chances, and you have a record of futility in big games at home that is striking.

The consensus seems to be that most of the current core position players (with the possible exception of Willson Contreras) will remain through next season, when many of them will be free agents. Contreras might be moved because he has substantial trade value, but it is unlikely the Cubs could get fair value in trades for players like Bryant or Schwarber. Given the "walk year" phenomenon, where players have a tendency to put up big numbers the season before they hit the free-agent market, there is at least some reason to hope the Cubs can make one more run at a championship. But that assumes they can patch together a starting rotation, with Lester and Quintana likely gone and no money to spend on reinforcements—and that Bryant, Baez, Rizzo, and Schwarber have big years. Beyond that last-gasp hope for another special season, the team that Theo Epstein and company built to win the World Series appears to have run its course. And the notion of a dynasty, which seemed so real four years ago, is now dissipating like late-fall smoke.

Moving On

EIGHT TEAMS MOVED on to the more familiar best-of-five LDS matchups. As has been the case the past few years after the Cubs were eliminated from the postseason, I had an immediate aversion to watching any more baseball. I told myself I just didn't care what happened from here on out. But, as it almost always is, this was a position I found hard to maintain because it is still *baseball*, often some of the best baseball of the year. There were still stories to play out, surprises to be sprung, heroes and goats to be made. Thus, as the divisional series began to unfold, I found myself repeatedly looking over my shoulder to see what was going on.

Of the four series, the two on the National League side were perfunctory affairs that barely commanded much of my attention. The Dodgers and Braves, the teams with the two best records in the league, dispatched the Padres and Marlins, respectively, in three games straight. In the final two games of the latter series, the Marlins did not manage to score a single run. One of the two American League series—Houston vs. Oakland—produced only slightly more suspense. The Astros' bats, which had been uncharacteristically quiet through the regular season, came to life. Even without the aid of a pitch-tipping mechanism, Houston scored 33 runs in the four games of their decisive 3–1 series win. Their only loss came in a game they led 7–4 before their bullpen yielded five runs in the seventh and eighth innings.

The final series of the four, between the New York Yankees and Tampa Bay Rays, was a more interesting story. The two teams could hardly be more different optically. The current Yankees squad is cut in the image of nearly a century of Yankee teams—funded by a huge budget and populated by big name players. The Yankees had the highest team payroll in baseball in 2020, and their roster includes several big stars and lots of familiar names: Giancarlo Stanton, Aaron Judge, Gerritt Cole, Aroldis Chapman, Glyber Torres, DJ LeMahieu, Masahiro Tanaka. The Rays, by contrast, had the fourth lowest payroll in MLB, roughly a quarter of New York's, and a roster most of whose names are familiar primarily to hard-core baseball fans. Beyond Blake Snell, who won the 2018 Cy Young, and the well-traveled veteran Charlie Morton, the Rays' key players were Randy Arozarena, Brandon Lowe, Ji-man Choi, Kevin Kiermaier, Joey Wendle, Manuel Margot, Tyler Glasnow, and Willy Adames. The starting lineup for the Yankees in Game 1 had a collective 14 All-Star seasons, while the Rays' lineup had two.

None of the first three games was a pitchers' duel, as the two teams put up a total of 12 runs in each game. Rather, they were home run battles in which the teams hit 16 long balls, including three each by Giancarlo Stanton for the Yankees and Randy Arozarena for the Rays. And the victory in each game went to the team that out-homered the other. Thus, Tampa Bay's nine home runs helped give them a 2–1 series lead.

Game 4 continued the pattern as home runs by Luke Voit and Glyber Torres were more than enough to secure a 5–1 win over the homerless Rays, who scored their lone run on a bases-loaded force out in the third inning. Aroldis Chapman closed out the game with a perfect ninth inning, striking out Mike Brosseau for the final out.

Game 5 was another story altogether—a well-pitched game in which each team managed only three hits. The Game 1 starters, Gerrit Cole and Tyler Glasnow, matched up again, and both were very good for as long as they were around. Glasnow left after 2 1/3 innings of work, having yielded no hits or runs and striking out the last batter he faced, with the game scoreless. Aaron Judge put the Yankees up 1–0 with a home run off Nick Anderson leading off the fourth inning, and Austin Meadows tied the game with a solo shot in the bottom of the fifth. Cole lasted one out into the sixth having yielded just a single hit—the home run by Meadows.

The game remained tied 1–1 going into the bottom of the eighth, and Yankees manager Aaron Boone brought in Aroldis Chapman to keep it that way. Chapman retired the first hitter he faced, Randy Arozarena, who figured to be the toughest out of the inning. Next up was Mike Brosseau, who had replaced Ji-Man Choi at first base in the sixth inning. Among the potential heroes for Tampa Bay in this spot, Brosseau probably would not have been high on the list. He has been a part-time player for the Rays for the last two seasons after they signed him as an undrafted free agent in 2016. But he had also homered three times against the Yankees during the regular season, so heroics were not beyond hope. Still, he was facing Chapman, who had fanned Brosseau for the 27th out the night before.

For 11 years in the big leagues, Chapman has been one of the hardest-throwing and most intimidating relievers in the game. Early in his career, he stood out for his ability to consistently deliver the ball at over 100 mph. Today, there are a number of pitchers who routinely hit three digits on the radar gun and Chapman may have lost a mile or two per hour on his heater, but he still throws very hard. In limited work in 2020 he struck hitters out at a rate of 17 per nine innings, which was the second highest rate of his career.

Brosseau had history with Chapman. In a game on September 1, Chapman had precipitated a bench clearing disagreement when he buzzed a high inside fastball that barely missed hitting Brosseau in the head. In making the final out of Game 4, Brosseau had hung tough against Chapman, striking out on the eighth pitch of the at bat after fighting off several tough pitches. And last night's at bat played out the same way. Brosseau fell behind quickly 0–2 but then took two pitches, one outside and one high, to even the count. He fouled off the next two pitches and took a 101-mph fastball that just missed the inside corner to run the count full. After spoiling two more Chapman pitches, announcer Ron Darling observed that "his swings are getting better and better." It was a prophetic comment. On the next pitch, the tenth of the at bat, Brosseau caught up with a 100-mph fastball and drove it over the left field fence to put the Rays ahead 2–1. Tampa Bay closer Diego Castillo, working his second inning of relief, retired the Yankees in order in the ninth to send the Rays to the ALCS for the second time in the team's history.

League Championships

B Y THE TIME the two League Championship Series began, with their familiar best-of-seven format, it became a little harder to remember just how strange this season had been—harder, but not impossible. The games were for the first time being played in neutral sites. And rather than the usual schedule of 2-3-2, with off days for travel, each series would proceed until finished with no off days. This promised to upend whatever might otherwise in 2020 be a normal starting pitching pattern.

Of the four remaining teams, three had the best regular season records in their respective leagues: the Dodgers, Braves, and Rays. And the fourth member of the quartet, the Astros, had won 107 games in 2019 and lost in the seventh game of the World Series. Except perhaps for the Astros, who had lost two of their top starters (one to injury and the other to free agency), it was hard to argue that any of the four were teams we would have been surprised to see here after a normal 162-game season. But for the overhanging pall of the pandemic, it looked very much like the prelude to the World Series in any other year.

October 14

BILLY BEANE IS quoted in *Moneyball* as saying. "My job is to get us to the playoffs. What happens after that is fucking luck." The Astros have done their best in the first three games against Tampa Bay to prove that. They came into this series having scored 33 runs and having hit 12 home runs in their four-game ALDS elimination of Oakland. In the first three games of this series, each of which they have lost, Houston hitters have tattooed the baseball. In the first two games alone, the Rays have made at least 10 outstanding defensive plays, including several by Kevin Kiermaier and Willy Adames, to take hits away from the Astros. In Game 2, Alex Bregman hit the ball really hard five times, and got no hits. The Astros had failed to follow the venerable advice of Wee Willie Keeler: "Hit 'em where they ain't."

Despite all the hard-hit outs, the Astros still managed to out-hit the Rays 26–18 in the first three games. One of the current favorite toys of hitting analytics, xBA, quantifies what we saw in those three losses to Tampa Bay—that the Astros hit the ball much harder than the Rays did and should have reached base even more times than they did. According to Statcast, their xBA in those three games—their statistically expected batting average based on the trajectory and exit velocity of the balls they put in play—was .320, .357, and .265, versus Tampa Bay's .190, .165, and .214. And yet, the Astros find themselves down 3–0, facing the nearly impossible task of winning four straight games to advance to the World Series.

Meanwhile, the Astros' star second baseman, Jose Altuve, has made three throwing errors in the past two games. The third of those errors, in Game 3 on an off-target toss to Carlos Correa at second to start a potential double play, prompted one of the TV commentators to speculate whether Altuve has "the thing." He did not elaborate, but many viewers understood. The thing, otherwise known by names such as the "disease" or the "yips," is a player's sudden loss of the ability to make an accurate throw, usually a short one. It happens most often to pitchers or catchers, but there is a small set of second basemen, Steve Sax and Chuck Knoblauch being the most notable, who have suffered from this affliction.

In 1983, the Dodgers' Steve Sax, 23 years old and coming off a season in which he had been Rookie of the Year in the National League, suddenly could not make the routine throw to first base with any consistency. Sax made 30 errors that year, many on errant throws. Chuck Knoblauch, like Sax, was the Rookie of the Year as a 22-year-old second baseman, for the Minnesota Twins. After his first seven seasons, Knoblauch had been an All-Star four times, won a Gold Glove at second base, and had a career .304 batting average. He was a star. But in his ninth major-league season, then playing for the New York Yankees, Knoblauch lost the ability to make the short throw to first base. During the 1999 season, he made 26 errors, more than any other second baseman. Of those 26 errors, 14 were on throws to first. Things got even worse for Knoblauch in 2000, when he had made 10 throwing errors before the all-star break. On June 16 of that year, after making three errors on routine throws in the first six innings, Knoblauch took himself out of the game. By the end of the season, he was playing almost exclusively as a DH, and the following year he was moved to left field.

Although he had a miserable 2020 season at the plate, Jose Altuve has been the best player on the Astros roster over the past decade and at age 30 is on a career path that could well put him in the Hall of Fame. He has consistently been an above-average defensive second baseman and has won one Gold Glove at that position. So it was surprising to see him show, even briefly, symptoms of the disease that had struck Chuck Knoblauch at the same age. It remains to be seen whether these three bad throws in rapid succession are indicative of something serious, or just an aberrational glitch. And it remains to be seen whether the hits will start falling in for the Astros before it is too late.

October 16

THE OPENING GAME of the NLCS matchup between Los Angeles and Atlanta was an excellent pitchers' duel most of the way. The starters, Walker Buehler and Max Fried, each gave up a solo home run (by Freddie Freeman for the Braves and Kiké Hernandez to square things for the Dodgers) before turning the game over to their bullpens. The game remained tied 1–1 through eight innings.

In the ninth, Blake Treinen, the Dodgers' fifth pitcher, gave up a leadoff home run to Austin Riley, 23 and in his second year with the Braves. Ronald Acuna followed with a double ripped to left, and Freddie Freeman hit a high drive to center, which was caught by Bellinger but advanced Acuna to third. That brought up Marcel Ozuna, a free agent acquisition who has been hugely productive for the Braves this year.

With Acuna dancing at third, itching to score, Ozuna was all uncontrolled energy at the plate, twitching and violently pantomiming swings between pitches. Anxious to bring Acuna in, he jumped at the first two pitches from Treinen, fouling both of them off, but he then found the discipline to lay off three straight breaking balls—away, then in, then away. Finally, after fouling off another pitch, Ozuna fisted a ball into open space in right to score Acuna. Ozzie Albies followed that up with a two-run shot to left center, and suddenly it was a 5–1 ball game. Mark Melancon, warming up in the Braves' bullpen, caught the Albies home run ball, then came in and retired the side in order in the bottom of the ninth to nail down the win.

In a season that has finally seen the unification (at least for now) of the two leagues' use of the designated hitter rule, this game reflected a new distinction between them: fans in the park. Petco Park in San Diego, where the ALCS is being played, has remained devoid of fans, like every other major-league park during the regular season and postseason so far this year, with the exception of inside-the-bubble family members allowed to attend in person. In Arlington, Texas, however, where the local authorities have been more open to large outdoor gatherings despite the Covid-19 pandemic, MLB has allowed up to 10,700 paying fans to attend the NLCS games being played in Globe Life Field. And the same will be true of the World Series. So there was a live crowd for this game, and, annoyingly, they started the "tomahawk chop" chant after the Dodgers made their first out in the bottom of the ninth. Maybe the carboard cutouts were better, after all.

The second game of this series was, in a couple ways, a prototypical 2020 baseball game: 14 pitchers were used, seven by each team, neither starter lasted five innings, and the game took four hours and 12 minutes to complete. What began as an apparent blowout, with the Braves up 7–0 going into the bottom of the seventh, turned into a nail-biter for Atlanta. The Dodgers closed the gap on a three-run Corey Seager home run in that inning, but they still trailed 8–3 after eight. In the bottom of the ninth, though, Mookie Betts singled, Seager doubled, and Max Muncy homered to make it 8–6. After an error by Ozzie Albies, Cody Bellinger tripled to right off closer Mark Melancon to make it an 8–7 game with the tying run now on third. Melancon, however, retired AJ Pollack on a ground ball to third to give the Braves a 2–0 series lead.

The next two games were in fact blowouts. In Game 3, the Dodgers roughed up two Braves pitchers for 15 runs in the first three innings, which allowed starter Julio Urias to retire for the day after five innings of stress-free work. The following night, it was the Braves' turn to beat up on Dodger pitching. Kershaw started for the Dodgers, and the game was tied 1–1 going into the bottom of the sixth. Kershaw had thrown 71 pitches and faced only 18 batters through five. But in the sixth, Acuna led off with a single, and Freeman and Ozuna followed with doubles. Brusdar Graterol replaced Kershaw, but the Braves kept on hitting, eventually putting up six runs in the inning. They added three more in the seventh and eighth and cruised to a 10–2 win. The Dodgers now need to win three straight games to get another chance for their first World Series win since 1988.

October 17

THIS ALCS HAS given us another baseball rarity: only once before in postseason play has a team fallen behind 3–0 and won the next three games to force a Game 7. The Boston Red Sox did that in the 2004 ALCS against the New York Yankees and then went on to make it four straight, beating the Yankees in the seventh game to move on to the World Series. Houston is now the second team to do so, having taken the last three games from Tampa Bay to even the series.

Houston won Games 4 and 5 by identical 4–3 scores. In Game 4, Altuve put the Astros up early with a solo home run in the first and then doubled in another run in the third. After Randy Arozarena tied the game with a two-run homer in the fourth, Houston took a 4–2 lead in the bottom of the fifth when George Springer answered with a two-run shot of his own. The Astros held on in the ninth after Willy Adames doubled in a run to close the gap but died at third as Yoshi Tsutsugo lined a ball to deep right center field that was caught for the final out to keep the Astros' hopes alive. Game 5 was an even tighter affair. Ji-Man Choi homered in the top of the eighth, the Rays' third solo home run of the game, to tie things at 3–3. That was how it stood with one out in the bottom of the ninth when Carlos Correa crushed a 1–1 pitch from Nick Anderson to deep center field for a walk-off home run, bringing the Astros a game closer.

While a best-of-seven series is a short span of time in baseball years, it can still be long enough for things to start to even out. Houston's line drives and grounders that repeatedly went either right at a Rays fielder, or on which one of them made a spectacular low-percentage catch, are now finding the holes and open outfield territory between fielders. That was most evident in Game 6, which the Astros won comfortably 7–4. Despite scoring the most runs of any game so far in the series, the Astros did so with a fairly anemic xBA of just .209. Although they did score one run on a solo homer by Kyle Tucker, most of their run production came on ground ball singles that found holes rather than Rays fielders, as in the first three games. Game 6 was also notable in that it was the first game of the series in which the tying or go-ahead run was not at the plate when the final out was recorded. But whatever Game 6 lacked in suspense was more than outweighed by the significance of the Astros tying the series at three games apiece.

Now, if Tampa Bay can beat Houston in Game 7 tonight after squandering their 3–0 series lead, they will become the first team in baseball history to accomplish that feat. It seems like a tall task; Houston has momentum and may simply be too good right now. Jose Altuve, the heart of the Astros' order, is hitting at a .454 clip for the series, has an OPS north of 1.400, and appears to have gotten past his defensive hiccups of Games 2 and 3. Of course, as Earl Weaver reminded us years ago, "momentum is only as good as tomorrow's starting pitcher." The Astros will have Lance McCullers pitching Game 7 against their former teammate, Charlie Morton. Morton has been very good in both of his postseason starts this year, while McCullers gave up all four of the Rays runs in Game 2 and was roughed up for eight hits and five runs in just four innings of work in his one ALDS start. So, we will see. However the game turns out, it will make baseball history.

THE DODGERS MAY not have faced quite as daunting a task as the Astros, but they did well to erase a 3–1 series deficit and force a Game 7 against the Braves. Game 5 was a bullpen game with the teams using 13 pitchers between them. This was quite clearly by design for Atlanta, when they removed A. J. Minter after three scoreless innings in which he gave up just one hit and struck out seven—though maybe by necessity for the Dodgers as starter Dustin May struggled through two innings in which he threw 55 pitches and spotted the Braves a 2–0 lead. Trailing 2–1, the Dodgers turned the game around in the sixth inning when catcher Will Smith hit a three-run homer off Atlanta pitcher . . . Will Smith. The Dodgers stretched their lead to 7–2 in the next inning when Mookie Betts singled home Chris Taylor, who had doubled, and Corey Seeger followed with a two-run homer. Atlanta scratched out one more run, but Kenley Jansen closed the game out decisively by striking out the side in the ninth.

Game 6 featured a rematch between Max Fried for the Braves and Walker Buehler for the Dodgers. Fried had one of those first innings that give pitchers nightmares. He gave up back-to-back home runs to Corey Seager and Justin Turner, followed by a single, a walk, and another single, by Cody Bellinger, to make it 3–0 after one. Fried settled down and pitched into the seventh without giving up another run, but it was too late. Buehler scattered seven hits over six scoreless innings before departing. The Braves scored a run in the seventh on a triple by Nick Markakis, who had initially opted out of the season due to Covid-19 concerns but later reconsidered and joined the team, and a double by Ronald Acuna. The Dodger bullpen slammed the door for the next two innings, though, as Kenley Jansen again pitched a 1-2-3 ninth. And so, like Houston and Tampa Bay, the Dodgers and Braves would play a double elimination game.

October 19

FOR A BASEBALL fan, back-to-back Game 7s in the ALCS and NLCS is about as good as it gets. And in a year of baseball (and other) deprivations, this seemed to be a lot to expect. But the Astros, Rays, Dodgers, and Braves managed to deliver us exactly that. It was the first season since 2004 that both league championship series have gone seven games.

The Astros and Rays were up first. The Rays took an early 3–0 lead after two innings, scoring the way they scored two-thirds of their runs in this series—with home runs. The surprising breakout star of the postseason, Randy Arozarena, hit a two-run homer in the first, his seventh of the postseason, and Mike Zunino followed with a solo shot in the second. Meanwhile, Charlie Morton was virtually unhittable. He did not yield his second hit until there were two outs in the sixth, at which point he was removed for reliever Nick Anderson. Tampa Bay pushed another run across in the bottom of the sixth on a single, walk, and two fly-outs. Houston now trailed by four, with nine outs left.

Houston's offense showed signs of life in the seventh against Anderson. Correa led off by crushing a line drive to right center, but it was caught for the first out. Bregman and Tucker then singled, but Yuli Guriel grounded into a double play to end the inning. In the eighth, the Astros threatened again when Anderson walked Aledmys Diaz, and Altuve singled with two outs. Pete Fairbanks replaced Anderson and promptly walked Michael Brantley on four pitches to load the bases. Carlos Correa then singled to right against the shifted infield, scoring Diaz and Altuve. The Astros now had the tying runs on base, with Alex Bregman coming up.

Bregman has been one of Houston's most productive hitters since he broke in at age 22 in 2016. In 2018 and 2019, he averaged over .290, had 88 doubles and 72 home runs, and contributed over 16 WAR. But 2020 was a down year for him, with a regular season slash line of .242/.350/.451, and he was struggling through the first six games of this series. He came to the plate in the eighth inning with only four hits in the ALCS, none for extra bases, giving him identical batting and slugging averages of .148. Bregman was clearly anxious to produce and quickly fell behind 1–2. He then chased a 100-mph fastball from Fairbanks that was at the shoulders and nearly a foot outside, striking out to end the inning. The Astros managed a one-out single in the ninth, but Fairbanks got the next two hitters to send Tampa Bay to the World Series.

––––––––––

THE DODGERS-BRAVES GAME 7 the next night was a classic—a taut, well-played game with an appropriately dramatic game-winning at bat. Neither starter stuck around for long. Dustin May, the 22-year-old who had started Opening Day for the Dodgers in place of sore-backed Clayton Kershaw, pitched just one inning, in which he allowed one run on two walks and a single by Marcel Ozuna. He was replaced in the second inning by fellow-starter Tony Gonsolin, who gave up a home run to Dansby Swanson leading off the inning to put Atlanta up 2–0. Ian Anderson, another 22-year-old, who had been excellent in his six starts as a rookie in 2020, started for the Braves and lasted three innings. In the third, he yielded two runs on a walk, a double by Max Muncy and a Will Smith single that scored both runners and tied the game.

Gonsolin continued working into the top of the fourth but departed after walking the first two batters and then allowing a single by Austin Riley to give Atlanta a 3–2 lead they carried into the bottom of the sixth. The lead could easily have been larger if not for two excellent defensive plays by the Dodgers. In the fourth, after Blake Treinen relieved Gonsolin, with men on second and third and no outs Nick Markakis hit a ground ball to Justin Turner. Swanson, the runner on third, broke for home but was caught in a rundown. Turner eventually tagged him out, then alertly did a pirouette and threw to Corey Seager to nail Riley attempting to advance to third. Treinen got the final out with no further damage. In the next inning, Freddie Freeman drove a ball to right on which Mookie Betts ran to the wall, timed his leap perfectly, and went over the top of the wall to take away a home run. It was the third outstanding, run-saving play by Betts in as many games.

A. J. Minter, who had pitched three brilliant innings to start Game 5, came on as the fourth Atlanta pitcher of the night in the sixth. Leading off the inning, pinch-hitter Kiké Hernandez drove Minter's eighth pitch deep to left center for a game-tying home run. With three innings to play and the score tied, this game had the feel of one that could easily come down to one big play or one mistake by either team.

Yet another young Dodger starter, Julio Urias, became their fifth pitcher of the night in the top of the seventh. Urias is only 23 but is already in his fifth year with the Dodgers. In 2016, as a 19-year-old rookie, he posted a 3.39 ERA in 15 starts. In a piece for *Vice* the next year, Mike Piellucci described him as "the most precocious pitching prospect since Felix Hernandez . . . a once-in-a-decade bauble." Urias missed much of the 2017 and 2018 seasons rehabbing from major surgery in June 2017 to repair the anterior capsule in his shoulder. Unlike Tommy John elbow reconstruction, from which pitchers now regularly return to their pre-injury form, the shoulder injury Urias needed repaired has a much lower rate of successful recovery. But Urias made it back, appearing in 37 games in 2019, posting an outstanding 2.49 ERA in mixed starting and relief duty, and he had a 3.27 ERA in 10 starts this season. Urias is not an overpowering pitcher; he depends on craft more than brute force. And maybe most importantly in a game that could turn on one mistake pitch, he gives up very few home runs.

Urias retired the Braves in order in the top of the seventh on a fly out and two popups. Chris Martin, who had retired Justin Turner for the final out in the bottom of the sixth, stayed in to pitch the bottom of the seventh for the Braves. In 18 innings in relief during the regular season, Martin had posted an ERA of 1.00 with a superb WHIP of 0.611. In his 39 appearances over the last two seasons, he had given up just two home runs. And he looked dominant as he struck out the first two batters he faced in the inning, Max Muncy and Will Smith.

That brought up 2019 National League MVP Cody Bellinger, who was hitting .167 for the NLCS after a subpar regular season. Joe Buck and John Smoltz, calling the game for Fox, noted Bellinger's history of poor postseason performance and what a disappointing season 2020 had been for him. But then Smoltz added, "One swing changes all that." Two pitches later, the eighth of the at bat, Martin put the ball over the heart of the plate and Bellinger crushed it to deep right field. Bellinger knew it instantly—he dropped the bat at the plate and then took six or seven deliberate steps toward first before starting his home run trot and preening to the Dodger dugout.

In a game that had been a seesaw battle, Braves fans might reasonably have expected a comeback, with six outs left and hitters like Freeman, Ozuna, and Albies coming up. But Julio Urias was simply too tough. He retired the Braves in order in the eighth and ninth to complete three perfect innings of relief. It was a performance reminiscent of Madison Bumgarner in Game 7 of the 2014 World Series when he pitched the final five innings of that game without allowing a run to preserve the Giants' 3–2 win.

Corey Seager, who hit five home runs and drove in 11 in the series was voted MVP. But Los Angeles had many heroes—from Cody Bellinger, Will Smith, and Kiké Hernandez, whose hits in Game 7 had the greatest impact on the outcome, to pitchers Kenley Jansen and Julio Urias, who pitched three perfect ninth innings to nail down the last three Dodgers' victories.

World Series

AFTER THE TWO highly entertaining seven-game League Championship series, the World Series had a feeling of anti-climax as it began. The first three games of the Series were largely free of thrills or much suspense.

In Game 1, the Dodgers tagged Tyler Glasnow for six runs in four and a third innings, the first two coming on a Cody Bellinger home run. Meanwhile, Clayton Kershaw gave up only two hits and a run before departing after six efficient innings of work, and the Dodgers cruised to an 8–3 win.

Game 2 was perhaps most interesting because the Dodgers took a page from the Rays' book and made it a "bullpen game." Starter Tony Gonsolin worked only an inning and a third (in which he gave up one run on one hit, a first inning solo homer), and he was followed by six other Dodger pitchers, each of whom contributed an inning or two. Blake Snell started for the Rays and worked into the fifth, giving up two runs while recording nine of his 14 outs via strikeout. The highlight for Tampa Bay was that their best hitter over the regular season, Brandon Lowe, broke out of a horrible postseason slump to hit two home runs. The Dodgers hit three long balls of their own, but it was too little too late, and the Rays won 6–4.

Game 3 was also largely without suspense, as the Dodgers jumped to an early 5–0 lead, Walker Buehler held the Rays to one run over six innings, and the Dodgers notched a comfortable 6–2 win.

October 25

THE TENOR OF the Series changed dramatically in Game 4. The reasons we love to watch baseball are many and varied. But one of them has to be the possibility we will see something special—something like last night's 8–7 win by Tampa Bay over the Los Angeles Dodgers. The probability of winning the game shifted from team to team a remarkable 10 times during the course of the game. This is 2020, and so the game's numerous twists of fortune featured six home runs, but also six runs scoring on old-fashioned singles, all with two out. And the unlikely outcome that unfolded in the ninth inning reflected one of the biggest shifts in win probability ever on the final play of a World Series game. It was only the third time in World Series history a team has come from behind to win with two outs in the bottom of the ninth.

Because it was not an elimination game (though it certainly had the feel of one), the Rays' win may not take its place alongside other World Series classics such as Boston's Game 6 win over Cincinnati in 1975, or its loss to the Mets in Game 6 of the 1986 Series, or the St. Louis Cardinals' wild 10–9, 11-inning win over Texas in 2011's Game 6, or

Game 7 of the 2016 World Series between Chicago and Cleveland. But if the Rays go on to win the Series, we can be sure that no fan of the Dodgers or Rays will ever forget this game. And if that is the result, Chris Taylor's misplay of Brett Phillips's single and Will Smith's whiff of the relay throw to the plate from Max Muncy will live in infamy alongside Bill Buckner allowing Mookie Wilson's ground ball to go between his legs or Curt Flood taking a fatal first step in on Jim Northrop's line drive that went over his head in Game 7 of the 1968 World Series.

Even before the wild finish, the Saturday night game, inning by inning, etched its place as a postseason classic. The scoring began with solo home runs by three of the biggest hitting stars of the Series so far. Justin Turner put the Dodgers ahead 1-0 with a home run in the first inning, the second straight game in which he had done that. And Corey Seager doubled the lead with a homer in the third, his eighth of the postseason. Not to be outdone, Randy Arozarena homered in the bottom of the fourth for his record-setting* ninth of the postseason. And these were just the warmup for what would follow.

Arozarena's home run in the fourth began a remarkable streak of eight consecutive half-innings in which the teams would score at least one run. (In a postseason in which extensive utilization of bullpens has been a big part of the story, this game was not a testament to the effectiveness of the parade of relievers. Of the 11 relief pitchers used in the game—six by the Rays and five by the Dodgers—eight of them gave up at least one earned run.) The Dodgers extended their lead in the top of the fifth when Max Muncy singled with two outs to drive home Corey Seager, only to have Tampa Bay close the gap again on another solo home run, this time by Hunter Renfroe leading off the bottom half. Dodgers starter Julio Urias departed with two outs in the fifth after striking out the last two Tampa Bay hitters he faced (his eighth and ninth strikeouts). In the sixth, the Dodgers pushed across another run on a Kiké Hernandez two-out double, but this time the Rays seized the lead 5–4 in the bottom of the sixth on a three-run homer by Brandon Lowe (his third home run in three games).

The Dodgers flipped the lead once more in the top of the seventh when pinch-hitter Joc Pederson came up with the bases loaded and lined a two-out single into right center against the heavily shifted Tampa Bay defensive alignment, scoring two runs. Although Statcast gave the ball a 96 percent chance of being a hit based on its trajectory and exit velocity, Brandon Lowe was positioned so perfectly in short right field that his leaping attempt got a glove on the ball and almost robbed Pederson of a near-sure hit. In the bottom of the inning, Kevin Kiermaier quickly evened the score, driving a solo home run deep into the right-center field stands.

To complete the scoring binge, Corey Seager delivered another big two-out hit in the top of the eighth (Seager's fourth hit of the game), blooping a ball off his fists into short left-center to score Chris Taylor and put the Dodgers back up 7–6. This prompted the Dodger bench to flash hand signals for what is apparently one of the team's mottos this season: "Barrels are overrated," an obvious reference to the current Statcast-driven obsession with hard-hit balls, and particularly those identified as having been hit "on the barrel."

That was how things stood as the bottom of the ninth inning began, with Kenley Jansen taking the mound for the Dodgers. Jansen has saved 330 regular and postseason games in his 11 seasons with the Dodgers and has been almost unhittable in several of those years. But he has not been dominant in the last two seasons, last year blowing eight of 41 save opportunities. Although he got 11 saves in 13 chances in this year's short season, critics still say he has lost both the command and velocity that have made him so effective for a decade. One who has continued to express complete confidence in Jansen—the person whose opinion counts most—is his manager, Dave Roberts. And he had clearly held him in the bullpen through numerous pitching changes for just this spot.

Jansen struck out the leadoff man, but then gave up a line-drive single to Kevin Kiermaier. A hard-hit deep fly to left by Joey Wendle brought the Dodgers within one out of a 3–1 Series lead. Next up was Randy Arozarena. Jansen plainly did not want to let Arozarena beat him with a long ball and eventually walked him in a tense seven-pitch at bat. This visibly irritated Arozarena, who wanted to hit, but it sent the tying run to second. As Brett Phillips stepped to the plate, Tampa Bay's statistical win probability according to Baseball-Reference.com was 19 percent. But in reality, their chances were even lower than that. In four major-league seasons, Phillips has a career .202 batting average, and this year he hit .150. He was hitless in his two prior at bats this postseason, both coming in the ALDS. But Kevin Cash's bench was empty, so the game hung on Tampa Bay's worst hitter.

What happened next was the stuff of nightmares for Dodger fans. After falling behind 1–2, Phillips was able to muscle a Jansen cutter into right center. Center fielder Chris Taylor, charging in and to his left, reached down to field the ball, but it bounced off his glove. Arozarena was running hard off the crack of the bat and never slowed down as he approached third, where coach Rodney Linares vigorously waved him home. As he rounded third, however, Arozarena stumbled and eventually tumbled about halfway between third and home. Meanwhile, Taylor had quickly chased down the ball and fired it toward the plate. Max Muncy cut off the throw, turned, and threw the ball to catcher Will Smith—who missed it. Arozarena had regained his feet and started back to third, but reversed direction again and slid home head-first with the winning run, ecstatically slapping the plate as bedlam erupted on the field around him.

Taylor's misplay (which was scored as an error) was totally unforced. As soon as Phillips's softly hit liner took two hops on the turf in right center, Taylor had to know that there was zero chance he was going to throw out Kiermaier at home. And with the speedy Arozarena running on contact with two outs, the chances of keeping him from taking third were exactly the same. The outcome was predetermined: game tied, runners at first and third. There was no reason to rush. All he had to do was field the ball cleanly and throw it to someone near second base. Instead, he went for a quick pick-and-throw move and booted the ball. Still, he recovered quickly, retrieving the ball and making a good throw. And Muncy did the right thing in cutting it off rather than letting Smith try to field what likely would have been a two-hopper all the way to the plate.

Smith's failure to catch the throw home (which was also charged as an error in a scorer's revision to the official box score the following morning) was also the result of unnecessary haste. He obviously either saw or sensed that Arozarena was coming home. But Smith probably didn't see him stumble to the ground after he rounded third as Smith turned to focus on the throw from Muncy. That throw, while not a bad one, was to the first base side of home. As the ball reached him, Smith clearly thought he was going to need to make a fast swipe tag to beat the runner to the plate. Either he took his eye off the ball briefly to see where Arozarena was or he started his move back toward the third base line a fraction of a second too soon. Either way, the ball clanked off the edge of his mitt and the winning run scored uncontested.

That final play of the game can be viewed in any of several ways: as a storybook tale of an unlikely hero, as a comedy of errors, as a triumph of aggressive base running over good judgment, or as just one more illustration that the pressure of the moment can make catching and throwing the ball difficult for even the game's best players. It is in the last two categories that this game falls within a small set of special postseason games—those in which the outcome turned on the ability of a team to make a throw under pressure to cut down an aggressive base runner with the game on the line.

In Game 7 of the 1992 NLCS, the Braves trailed the Pirates by a run with two outs in the bottom of the ninth but had the bases loaded. Pinch hitter Francisco Cabrera lined a single to left, toward Gold Glove winner Barry Bonds. The runner on second was Sid Bream, one of the slowest men in baseball. Third base coach Jimmy Williams, apparently unintimidated by Bonds' arm and Bream's woeful lack of speed, waved him home. Bonds took four steps to his left, fielded the ball cleanly, and threw toward the plate. The throw was well to the first base side of home. Catcher Mike LaValliere made a fine play to backhand the ball on one hop, but his diving swipe tag was a split second late, and Bream was safe. A good throw was going to get Bream easily—the replay shows that LaValliere had the ball in his mitt just as Bream was beginning his slide, still a good 15 feet from the plate. But Bonds didn't make a good throw, and what should have been a sure out to send the game into extra innings turned into the winning run sending the Braves to the World Series.

A similar scene played out in Game 5 of the 2015 World Series between the Kansas City Royals and the New York Mets. The Royals. who led the Series three games to one, trailed by a run in the ninth inning with Eric Hosmer on third and one out. The next batter, Salvador Perez, hit a broken-bat grounder to the left side. Mets third baseman David Wright cut the ball off in front of shortstop Wilmer Flores. With his momentum carrying him toward the mound, Wright looked over his shoulder to freeze Hosmer before making the throw to first. As soon as Wright turned back toward first base, Hosmer broke for the plate. He went on his own. It was an aggressive, if not reckless, play. Mets first baseman Lucas Duda took the perfect throw from Wright to retire Perez and had time to come home to complete a game-ending double play and send the Series to Game 6.

But Hosmer had caught Duda by surprise, and he rushed his throw. Although the throw beat Hosmer to the plate, it was well up the first base line, out of the catcher's reach, and Hosmer slid home safely to tie the score. The Royals went on to win the game—and their first World Series in 30 years—in the twelfth inning.

And then there is the throw that was not made, because it didn't have to be. In Game 7 of the 2014 World Series, San Francisco led Kansas City 3–2 in the ninth inning, with Madison Bumgarner working in his fifth inning of relief. With two outs and nobody on, Alex Gordon hit a line drive single to left-center field. Giants center fielder Gregor Blanco charged the ball, but misplayed the short hop, allowing the ball to roll to the wall where left fielder Juan Perez kicked it once before eventually picking it up and throwing it in to shortstop Brandon Crawford. Gordon, who is fast, was going at full speed as he rounded second. But as he approached third, with the ball on its way to Crawford in short left, third base coach Mike Jirschele raised his arms, then pointed emphatically at the bag, and Gordon stopped there. Watching the game, statistician and baseball analyst Nate Silver tweeted, "You send Gordon, and it's one of the 5 greatest baseball moments ever, regardless of whether he scores." But he didn't, and so it wasn't. With Gordon standing at third, the next batter, Salvador Perez, popped out to give Bumgarner the final out and San Francisco the World Series.

At the beginning of this season I wrote that, notwithstanding the imperfect nature of a 60-game schedule and revamped postseason format, I still looked forward to baseball being played because it offered, every day, "opportunities for something special, even unique, to happen." Had Alex Gordon tried to score in the ninth inning of Game 7 in 2014, a good, accurate throw from Crawford almost certainly would have nailed him at the plate, just as Randy Arozarena was almost certainly going to be out. But as players from Barry Bonds to Lucas Duda have proven—and as we saw again last night—the throw and catch necessary to retire a runner at the plate are not always made under the pressure of a potentially game-ending play. And that uncertainty, that ever-present human fallibility of the players—from Bill Buckner, to Barry Bonds, to Will Smith—is just one of the things that makes the game occasionally so surprising and memorable.

October 26

LAST NIGHT WAS a perfectly normal, reasonably suspenseful, pivotal Game 5. The Dodgers came out on top 4–2 because they got a couple big hits when they needed them, including two more home runs; Clayton Kershaw was just good enough for the 21 batters he faced, while Tyler Glasnow struggled to find a rhythm to go with his 100-mph stuff; and Dave Roberts's pitching plan worked pretty close to perfection. It was a well-played game (except for another error by Chris Taylor) in which, unlike the night before, nothing crazy happened. Well, almost nothing. Isn't it a little bit crazy that the most important pitch Kershaw threw was not an actual pitch? And at least a little strange that, for the second night in a row, an important part of the game was aggressive, maybe reckless, base running?

In an October 15 piece in *The Athletic*, Joe Posnanski wrote about 10 basic "tenets" of baseball from when he was growing up that "now seem silly, obsolete or quaint depending on your viewpoint." Tenet Five on his list was: "Be aggressive on the base paths." Thus, he notes, base stealing has declined dramatically, part of the overall view that risking an out by trying to steal a base or stretch a single into a double is simply not worth it. Related was Tenet Four: "The triple is the most exciting play in baseball." Consistent with the views on being aggressive generally, Posnanski says that, under the new thinking, it "just doesn't make sense to go for the triple and get yourself thrown out."

Posnanski's list of discarded conventional wisdom pretty accurately describes the state of baseball thinking in the era of the new analytics, which is what made Game 5 just a little crazy. Picking up from the way the Saturday night game ended, last night's game was a throwback to an era when taking an extra base (now a subcategory of what is derisively or longingly, depending on your viewpoint, referred to as "small ball") was a central part of the game.

In the first inning, Mookie Betts led off with a double and scored on a single by the still-hot Corey Seager. After Justin Turner struck out, Max Muncy came to the plate. Glasnow, who was struggling with his command, bounced one in the dirt that kicked no more than six feet in front of catcher Mike Zunino. Seager broke for second and beat the throw by a whisker—close enough for the Rays to ask for a review that allowed the safe call to stand. After Muncy walked and Will Smith whiffed for the second out, with Bellinger at the plate Glasnow threw a low inside pitch that bounced off the home plate umpire's shin guard just in front of the plate.

Seager had taken a large secondary lead off second and was able to sprint safely to third. Bellinger then reached on an infield single that allowed Seager to score only because he had advanced to third with his aggressive base running, as Chris Taylor struck out to end the inning.

With the Rays trailing 3–2 in the bottom of the fourth (after Yandy Diaz had tripled(!) and later scored the Rays' second run in the prior inning), Manuel Margot single handedly made his own case for the return of small ball. Margot led off the inning with a walk. Apparently not having received the memo that base-stealing is passe, he took off for second on Kershaw's first pitch to Hunter Renfroe. Chris Taylor, playing second base in this game, tried to bring the tag down before he had the ball and it bounced away. After a brief hesitation, again eschewing the new learning that risky base running is out of favor, Margot popped to his feet and took off for third. Taylor retrieved the ball and made a good throw, but Margot was called safe, and video review confirmed the call.

A pop up, walk, and strikeout later, Margot still stood on third. On an 0–1 count to Kevin Kiermaier, as Kershaw went into his signature long, deliberate stretch, hands slowly rising high above his head, Margot broke for home. Kershaw could not see this, but first baseman Max Muncy alertly yelled for Kershaw to step off. He did, without hesitation, and then quickly, but with no sense of panic, threw the ball hard to his catcher Austin Barnes. The throw was about shoulder high, and just to the first base side of the plate. Barnes made a sure-handed grab and quickly plunged both hands together into the path of the headfirst sliding Margot, who attempted to hook his left hand around the tag. The call was "out." There was no review, though from several angles it looked like he might have been safe.

A couple of people I know who watched the game have said they thought it was foolish for Margot to try to steal home because the odds were so heavily against him. But I don't think that is right. Margot was the tying run in what was shaping up to be a tight game. There were two outs with the left-handed hitting Kiermaier, a lifetime .248 hitter, at the plate. Kershaw had just struck out the last hitter on three pitches, and he was ahead of Kiermaier 0–1 (thereby reducing his effective batting average). In that situation, Margot's chances of scoring were well under 30 percent.

What about his chances of successfully stealing home? It's not like he was out easily. He came within the length of about two knuckles on his left hand of being safe. He got such a good jump that, if the Dodgers had been anything other than perfect in their execution—if Muncy had yelled "Home! Home!" about five hundredths of a second later, or if Kershaw had been just that much slower in stepping off the rubber, or if he had rushed and made a slightly worse throw, or if he had balked, or if Barnes had done what Will Smith did the night before—Margot was going to score.

And then there is history. The last player to successfully execute a straight steal of home in the World Series was Jackie Robinson 65 years ago against the Yankees in the 1955 World Series. And it was just as close as the play last night. Has there been a long string of failed attempts since then? No. According to Jayson Stark with the help of STATS, only one other player has attempted a straight steal of home in the World Series since Robinson in 1955 (and before last night)—Lonnie Smith, with two outs in the third inning of Game 6 of the 1982 World Series between St. Louis and Milwaukee. Don Sutton, a right hander, was on the mound, but he was pitching out of the windup. Smith broke for the plate, and Sutton delivered the pitch without breaking his motion and balking. Ted Simmons caught the pitch and applied the tag, and Smith was called out in a very close play—close, but almost certainly called wrong. The replay showed that Smith's hand got to the plate before Simmons tagged him. (There was no video review available then.)

Given how close these three plays were, when a runner on third knows what he is doing, picks the right spot and gets a good jump, the straight steal of home seems like a coin flip, and very likely better than the chance of scoring that runner with two outs otherwise. Margot's attempt was, on every level, a play you have to love.

October 28

THE 2020 BASEBALL season—the strangest, the most fraught, and in many ways the most controversial season ever—is over. It came to an end not with the loud bang of a home run or with the winning run sliding across the plate in a cloud of dust; not on a sparkling defensive play or on an egregious error; not on a mighty swing and miss; but instead, quietly, as the final two Tampa Bay hitters watched strike three cut through the heart of the strike zone without moving their bats. Just as he had done in Game 7 of the NLCS when he pitched three perfect innings to close out the game, Julio Urias, who had thrown 80 pitches in his Game

4 start, was again flawless. He retired all of the seven hitters he faced to nail down the Dodgers' Series-clinching 3–1 win.

Many would say the game ended well before these final at bats against the brilliant young Dodgers pitcher. They would say it ended when Tampa Bay manager Kevin Cash reached the top step of the dugout with one out in the bottom of the sixth inning and raised his right hand to call for relief pitcher Nick Anderson to come in for starter Blake Snell with the Rays ahead 1–0. (The Rays had taken that lead in the first inning on yet another home run by the amazing Randy Arozarena, his tenth of the postseason.) At that point, Snell had thrown 73 pitches, yielded two singles, struck out nine Dodger hitters and walked none, and he had dominated the hot hitting batters at the top of the Dodgers' lineup.

This was not a decision over which Cash hesitated. It was clear that as soon as Austin Barnes dropped his single into center field in front of Kevin Kiermaier and became just the second Dodgers hitter to reach base, Snell was done. Snell had apparently crossed some line that the Tampa Bay analytics brain trust drew before he threw his first pitch of the game. Removing him appeared to be as automatic as it was when Dave Roberts pulled Clayton Kershaw in the sixth inning of Game 5 after he retired the 20th and 21st batters he faced on two pitches. The Dodgers' plan going into that game was for him to face 21 batters, and they stuck to the plan. (It was the third consecutive postseason game in which Kershaw had faced exactly 21 batters.)

It is hardly unusual for a manager to signal a pitching change from the safety of the dugout steps before ever reaching the mound. There are several reasons for this. One, it is not easy to look in the eyes of a player who is pitching his heart out, one who is not obviously gassed and ready to go sit on the bench, and tell him he is done. It is far easier to take the ball when he is already officially out of the game. Second, a manager who has analyzed the situation and come to what he thinks is the best conclusion does not want to argue with his pitcher, and he certainly doesn't want to risk been talked out of the right decision. Sometimes, though, there are good reasons to wait until reaching the mound to make the decision. It affords the manager the opportunity to ask his catcher whether the pitcher has anything left, shifting that dirty work to a guy who does dirty work for a living. And it allows him to take the measure of his pitcher up close or listen to just how he intends to get the next guy out. But in the current analytical world of the Rays (like the Dodgers and most other major-league teams these days), there is little room for that kind of in-the-moment judgment.

Cash's explanation after the game in response to Ken Rosenthal's question about the decision was remarkable: "Snell had done everything we could have asked of him." Really? Blake Snell, who won the Cy Young award in 2018, is the ace of the Rays' staff. He is 27 years old, and he was pitching on full rest. Essentially, Cash seemed to be saying that in today's game the most a manager can ask of his number one starter, even when he is at his very best, is 73 pitches and 18 batters of scoreless pitching. Or maybe he was saying that that is the most he could expect of *this* pitcher.

In Cash's defense, Snell was certainly not a favorite to throw a complete game, or probably anything close to that. In his six-year major-league career, Snell has started 108 games and not completed a single one of them. In his 2018

Cy Young-winning season, when he had an ERA of 1.89, Snell started 31 games and threw 180 2/3 innings, an average of under six innings per start. And in this short season, he had not completed six innings once. But given how he was throwing, and his still low pitch count, was it unreasonable to expect another few outs from him? In going to Nick Anderson, Cash was not exactly playing a hot hand. Anderson had given up runs in both of his prior World Series appearances, as he had in each of the three games in which he appeared in the ALCS.

Regardless, Cash made the move, and before he had even returned to the dugout, the Twitterverse exploded in a flurry of expressions from fans and seasoned baseball analysts alike that this was one of the dumbest moves they had ever seen. It did not take long for Cash's decision to backfire. The first batter Anderson faced, Mookie Betts, ripped a double down the left field line, sending Barnes to third. On his second pitch to the next hitter, Corey Seager, Anderson threw one to the backstop, scoring Barnes to tie the game and sending Betts to third. The Rays pulled their infield in, but when Seager hit the next pitch to first baseman Ji-man Choi, Betts got a great jump and (just as he had done in a similar situation on Opening Day of the season) was able to beat the throw home. Anderson had thrown six pitches, and the Dodgers had a lead they would not relinquish.

———

THE DECISIONS WHETHER and when to take a pitcher out of the game collectively must give rise to the most second guessing of any a manager makes over the course of his career. When that decision is made in a critical game of the postseason and the outcome is not good, it can live on in the memories of baseball fans for decades. And, while this is not a data-based conclusion, I would bet that the majority of the second-guessed decisions involve those when the manager *failed* to make a pitching change. Here, it is not clear that it is fair to second-guess Cash at all, given that he may simply have been following a plan transmitted to him from above.

Ironically, given the collective outrage over what appeared to be Cash's mechanistic data-driven decision to pull Snell, one of the most excoriated managerial pitching decisions in recent memory resulted from a manager ignoring the data in deference to his gut reliance on a Hall of Fame pitcher. In 2003, before they had broken the Curse of the Bambino, the Boston Red Sox were playing the New York Yankees in Game 7 of the ALCS. It had been a great seesaw series, and the final game featured a matchup of Pedro Martinez against Roger Clemens. Martinez, who was 31, had had a phenomenal season. He led the league in both ERA and WHIP for the fifth time in his last seven seasons. In this game, the Yankees had touched Martinez for a solo home run in the seventh, but the Red Sox still led 5–2 going into the bottom of the eighth. He had thrown 100 pitches.

Although Martinez was about to face the top of the Yankees lineup for the fourth time, Boston manager Grady Little sent him back out to pitch the eighth. Martinez retired the first hitter on a popup, but Derek Jeter then doubled to right and Bernie Williams singled to drive home Jeter. Little went to the mound but made no motion to his bullpen, where Alan Embree was warmed up. At that point,

Martinez had thrown 115 pitches. (This was hardly unprecedented for Pedro. He had thrown more than 105 pitches 10 times that season, and he had thrown 130 in Game 1 of the ALDS.) Little asked Martinez if he had enough left to get the next batter, Hideki Matsui. Martinez was one of the best pitchers of all time, and also one of the proudest. So, of course he answered in the affirmative, and Little left him in the game. Matsui promptly hit a ground rule double down the right field line, and Jorge Posada followed with another double. With the game now tied, Little finally went to his bullpen, which stopped the bleeding. The Yankees eventually won the game 6–5 on Aaron Boone's walk-off home run in the bottom of the eleventh inning.

As critics of Little were quick to point out, in at bats against Martinez after he passed the 105-pitch mark, opposing hitters were batting .370. And both Boston's front office and Little were aware of the falloff in performance after his pitch count got much above 100. Theo Epstein, Boston's young general manager at the time, was a believer in analytics, and the Red Sox had brought on Bill James, an early and vocal advocate of sabermetrics, as an advisor to the team that season. The front office had shared their analytics insights with Little, but he wasn't really interested in the data; by his own admission, he preferred to play "educated hunches." And in this case, his educated hunch was that he had a better chance with a tired Pedro Martinez than a fresh reliever who'd had just a so-so season as a setup man. Although Epstein was unwilling to tie it to this one outcome, after the season Little was fired.

More recently, in the 2015 World Series, New York Mets manager Terry Collins incurred the wrathful second guessing of Mets fans when he allowed starter Matt Harvey to begin the ninth inning of what turned out to be the deciding game against the Kansas City Royals. Kansas City led the Series three games to one, but the Mets held a 2–0 lead in Game 5. Harvey was pitching a gem, allowing only four hits and striking out nine through eight innings on 102 pitches. The Mets' excellent closer, Jeurys Familia, had warmed up and it seemed certain that Collins was going to send him out to pitch the ninth inning. But television coverage of the dugout between innings showed Harvey engaged in animated discussion with Mets pitching coach Dan Warthen, and even amateur lip readers could see Harvey uttering the words "No way." Harvey then moved down the dugout to where Collins was standing and continued to plead his case. He prevailed, and after the Mets were retired in the bottom of the eighth, Harvey went back to the mound to finish the job. This was clearly an exception to the rule that the manager, not the pitcher, decides when a starter has had enough.

The ninth inning unraveled quickly for Harvey. He walked Lorenzo Cain, who led off the inning, and then gave up a double to Eric Hosmer that scored Cain. With the tying run on second, Collins came out to get Harvey and called for Familia. The Royals tied the game that inning and went on to clinch the Series with five runs in the twelfth inning. After the game, Collins explained that the original plan had been to bring in Familia after the seventh. But with Harvey looking so strong, Collins decided to give him another inning. Then, after the eighth, Collins was prepared to call on Familia, but Harvey was adamant about wanting to finish the game and Collins said that when he "looked in this kid's eyes . . . I just trusted him." Collins acknowledged he had one of the best closers in the game ready and should have put him in, but "sometimes you let your heart dictate your mind."

Back to the 2003 Martinez decision; is that what Grady Little did—let his heart overrule his mind? Maybe, but revisiting the decision in 2018 with the benefit of more recent analytical tools, sabermetrician Ben Lindberg, writing for *The Ringer*, concluded it was not so obvious Little had made the wrong decision. What the data shows is that Pedro Martinez, even at reduced effectiveness, was just as effective a pitcher facing a lineup for the fourth time as the warmed-up reliever Alan Embree was coming out of the bullpen. Lindberg also notes that Tom Tippett, another baseball probabilist, ran thousands of simulations and concluded the Red Sox had roughly an 80 percent win probability with either Martinez or Embree in the game to face Matsui. And, analyzing Martinez's pitch selection and inning-by-inning velocity over the game, Tippett concluded "Grady was right to think that Pedro still had plenty in the tank." In the end, the sabermetric conclusion is that the Red Sox had a *slightly* better chance with Embree in, but it was certainly not irrational—or in blatant conflict with the data—for Little to trust his gut and stick with Pedro.

IN THEIR POSTGAME discussion of this year's Game 6, Fox commentators Alex Rodriguez and David Ortiz both inveighed against the Snell decision as a glaring example of how "cybermetrics" was ruining baseball. But that really doesn't seem fair. Bill James, in discussing what led him to develop his analytical approach to the game, explained it this way: "It was never my idea that we needed to look more carefully at baseball statistics because statistics are the best way to look at baseball. It was my point, rather, that people do make judgments about baseball players primarily by statistics, not should but *do*, and because they *do*, they need a better understanding of what those statistics really mean."

The book *Moneyball* recounts how Billy Beane used analytics to find a way to win on a limited budget. After listening to one of his assistants explain what the statistics "really mean," he concluded that an overlooked metric—on-base percentage—was a key to identifying underpriced but productive players. Similarly, baseball front offices who looked at years' worth of data discovered that, over the long haul of a season, their teams would score more runs if they did not sacrifice an out to move up a base runner, and they acted on that knowledge. If the argument is that application of knowledge is ruining the game, it seems like there has to be a better fix than simply urging a return to ignorance.

The reality is that not only how teams view and use their pitchers, but the pitchers themselves have changed. A mechanical application of the principle that pitchers do worse the longer they stay in isn't the only explanation for why pitching is so different today. It is inconceivable that in 1968, when he averaged 8 2/3 innings per start, threw 13 shutouts and posted a 1.12 ERA, any of today's analytical models would have said it made sense to take Bob Gibson out of the game after six innings. Pitchers like Roger Clemens and Greg Maddux, or more recently Roy Halladay and Justin Verlander, demonstrated that they could pitch deep into games, and so they often did. Most of today's pitchers have not, and there are several reasons for this. They are almost never allowed by major-league managers to attempt it, in part because their training in the minor leagues does not prepare them for it. The quality of today's hitters has also made it that much more difficult to get them out repeatedly over the course of a game, and the prevalence of more batters working deep counts means throwing more pitches in fewer innings. Finally, teams are more focused on the phenomenon of "pitcher abuse" and are unwilling to risk damaging high-value arms through overuse, especially when managers have so many good hard-throwing relievers available in the bullpen.

Whatever the reasons for the difference in today's pitchers, it would almost never be the right call to leave Blake Snell in to pitch the eighth or ninth inning of an important game because he has never shown he is capable of doing it. And this becomes a self-perpetuating cycle when even baseball's best young pitchers are not being asked to give their team more than six solid innings. Perhaps, if pitchers developed the ability to do a better job of fooling hitters the third time they saw them in a game, the numbers would not scream so loudly in the ears of managers and front offices to take them out of there before the hitters get that third look.

The game played by those in the eight other positions on the field has not changed nearly as dramatically as the pitching game. Certainly, there are more home runs being hit overall, fewer singles and stolen bases, and more strikeouts. And widespread use of defensive shifting has altered how fielders are positioned in the field. But the five-tool players of today—players like Mike Trout or Mookie Betts—do not play a game that is fundamentally different from that of Willie Mays and Mickey Mantle. Barring injury, today's top hitters go to the plate 600-700 times a season and the best produce results roughly in line with decades of great players before them. (Mantle's career OBP was .421 and Trout's for his first 10 years is .418; Mays slugged .557 for his career and Trout so far is slugging .582.) Fifty home runs, 200 hits, 150 RBI are as much hitting milestones in today's game as they were 60 years ago. But the pitching game of today is almost unrecognizable compared to the game of just 30 years ago. How do you compare pitchers of today with those of a generation or two earlier? Do you argue that Shane Bieber at age 25 is just as good for the first five innings as Tom Seaver was at that age?

It does absolutely no good for septuagenarian fans like me to pine longingly for the feats of our pitching heroes of the past. Those days are gone. We have just finished watching Pitching Present (and likely Future) in this World Series, when 50 percent of the innings pitched were by pitchers out of the bullpen, and not a single starter worked past the sixth inning. But that does not mean we cannot appreciate what those pitchers did—and what, on rarer occasions, a few still do. That the pitching game has changed so much only makes us admire all the more accomplishments like Max Scherzer's in 2015 when he threw three shutouts in which he made 334 pitches, gave up a total of *one* hit, and struck out 43 hitters—or his 20-strikeout game the following year. And even more recently, we had Gerrit Cole's 15-strikeout, 118-pitch performance over 7 1/3 innings in Game 2 of the 2019 ALDS.

The changes in the pitching game also should not prevent us from revering performances like Jack Morris's 10-inning masterpiece that secured the Twins' 1–0 victory in Game 7 of the 1991 World Series. After the ninth inning of that game, with Morris having thrown about 120 pitches and working on three-days' rest, Twins manager Tom Kelly told him that he was done and that Rick Aguilera was coming in. Morris simply refused to accept it, telling Kelly "I'm not coming out of the game." Kelly turned to his pitching coach Dick Such and implored him to "tell him he's done"—to which Such reportedly responded with a line that could have been uttered by Richard Farnsworth's Red Blow in *The Natural*: "He's going pretty good, Skip." (Does that line ever get spoken in today's dugouts?) It was a different time, so Kelly told Morris to "go get 'em." And he did. Morris's catcher Brian Harper said Morris was as strong in the 10th as he'd been all night, and Harper "felt like he could have thrown 15 innings." He didn't have to, as the Twins scored in the bottom of the tenth.

This year, we lost the great Bob Gibson, one of the fiercest competitors ever to take the mound. In Game 1 of the 1968 World Series, Gibson threw a complete game shutout against the Detroit Tigers, one of the three complete games he threw in that Series, striking out 17 Tigers hitters. His book *Pitch by Pitch* describes, just as its title suggests, each pitch Gibson threw in that game—all 142 of them. It was the 27th ninth inning he had pitched that season, and his ERA for those 27 innings was 0.69. It is hard to imagine any closer could have done better.

Gibson frankly concedes that as he began the ninth inning that October day, "I was tuckered." And Gibson understood what happened to his delivery when he was tired, but he also knew how to compensate for that in the pitches he threw and how he threw them. He describes how, for him, the eighth inning was always the hardest, "and what made it the hardest inning was that it preceded the ninth. I always knew that if I could make it into the ninth, I'd be in position to finish the game, so I poured everything into the twenty-second, twenty-third, and twenty-fourth outs." Gibson emptied the tank in the eighth *in order to be able to pitch one more inning.* In the ninth inning of this game, Gibson struck out the side, including Al Kaline (another Hall of Famer who left us this year) for the third time and, finally, Willie Horton with a perfect slider that started at Horton's thigh and broke over the inside corner for a called strike three and the 27th out.

THE FINAL CODA to the season almost seems to have been inevitable, because it involves a Covid-19 controversy. Dodger third baseman Justin Turner left the game in the eighth inning because, earlier in the game, the Dodgers were informed that he had tested positive for Covid-19. MLB ordered that he immediately isolate himself from the rest of the team. And he did so, until the Dodgers won the Series. Then, although instructed by MLB not to do so, Turner joined the melee of the celebration on the field. A representative of MLB asked him to leave, and Turner refused.

Those leaping to Turner's defense point out that he had been in contact with his teammates throughout the game, and so there was little harm in any marginal additional exposure. This ignores that it was not just the players on the field, but wives, children, Dodger management, members of the media, and representatives of MLB—some of whom may well have fallen into the category of those at higher risk to the effects of a Covid-19 infection. That appeared either not to have occurred to Turner, or not to matter, as reflected in his failure to wear a mask much of the time he was mingling with the crowd on the field.

Critics of Turner's behavior have noted that millions of Americans have made sacrifices to protect others from exposure to the virus—foregoing wedding, birthday and anniversary celebrations; funeral services; dining in restaurants; and just gathering with friends. Of course, for most of those situations, people have had months, or at least days, to come to grips with their deprivations. Turner learned that he was to be isolated roughly 30 minutes before the biggest moment of his baseball life. So perhaps allowing his euphoria in that moment to overcome his good judgment is understandable and even excusable, but it is hard to say the same for his unwillingness to take the most modest of measures to reduce the chances of infecting those around him.

AND SO, ON that final note, baseball moves into a winter of uncertainty. Major League Baseball and the franchises that comprise it are uncertain about when and how they will be able to play in the spring. Will there be fans attending games; will there be revenue? Players without contracts or ones with team options are uncertain whether their team or any other will commit significant dollars to sign them in the current environment. And fans must wait 'til next year to see whether our "national pastime" will return to some semblance of normalcy. Or for that matter, whether life as we know it in this country will begin to move back in that direction.

Acknowledgments

THIS BOOK CULMINATED from a blog I decided to start at the beginning of the 2020 pandemic season to record my experience of baseball this year and share my reactions with a few other baseball fans. The first to read my early posts were my adult children, Alex and Katie, who are also lifelong baseball fans and gave me the initial encouragement I needed to keep on writing. Their support along the way has been invaluable. A handful of friends and fellow baseball followers, including Phil Beck, Mike Foradas, Bill Kayatta, and Peter Byrne, also were generous enough with their time to read and comment on some of my posts, and by doing so they allowed me to convince myself that at least someone might be interested in what I was writing. I am grateful to you all.

Special thanks to Jeff Given, who has been reading my occasional baseball writings for years and always provides his frank and helpful reactions. On this project, he was both a regular reader of my posts and a constant source of encouragement to keep generating new entries and later to pursue this book. I am most grateful for his feedback and helpful suggestions, though he is responsible for none of the shortcomings in this final product.

I want to thank my editor Dory Mayo for her professionalism, patience, and diligence in trying to impose some consistency and coherence on my manuscript. I also want to express my appreciation to Colin Rolfe at Epigraph Publishing for his excellent design work and assistance, and Paul Cohen for his initial encouragement to pursue this book.

I owe a huge debt to all of the great baseball writers, past and present, whose work has immeasurably enhanced my knowledge and appreciation of the game. Their writing, whether in books, essays, newspaper articles, or online posts, has been a source of inspiration. The list of names of all these accomplished baseball scribes is far too long to recount here but begins with Roger Angell, whose *New Yorker* baseball essays I first read in the early 1970s, decades of excellent articles by Peter Gammons and Tom Boswell, classics such as George Will's *Men at Work* and Daniel Okrent's *Nine Innings*—and more recently the books of the current generation of wonderful baseball writers such as Tyler Kepner, Jane Leavy, Jeff Passan, Ben Reiter, Travis Sawchick, and Tom Verducci. Thank you to all of the writers at *The Athletic*, SI.com, MLB.com, and all the other daily sources of interesting and insightful baseball writing—and especially writers like Jared Diamond, Joe Posnanski, and Jayson Stark, whose appreciation for the game seems to know no bounds.

There is another whole category of baseball commentators whose work has changed the way I look at and understand the game: that collection of analysts and writers who fall under the loose category of sabermetricians. Foremost among these is Bill James, whose eye-opening and fascinating iterations of the *Bill James Baseball Abstract* I began reading in the early 1980s. Others in this genre include John Thorn and Pete Palmer (whose book *The Hidden Game of Baseball* should be read by every serious fan), Jay Jaffe, Rany Jazayerli, Michael Lichtman, Ben Lindberg, Mike Petriello, and Tom Tango. Publications such as *Baseball Prospectus*, FanGraphs, and BaseballSavant have been invaluable sources of new ways to think about virtually all aspects of the game.

Finally, this book would not have been possible without the greatest resource for baseball information in existence: Baseball-Reference.com. It is impossible to overstate the number of times I turned to this source for historical information, to unearth stories, to flesh out details, and to gain insights about the players and games discussed in this book.

CPSIA information can be obtained
at www.ICGtesting.com
Printed in the USA
BVHW071529040321
601713BV00006B/687